sewing

projects in an afternoon®

sewing

projects in an afternoon®

SUSAN E. MICKEY

Sterling Publishing Co., Inc.
New York

Prolific Impressions Production Staff

Editor: Mickey Baskett
Creative Design: Susan E. Mickey
Photography: Jerry Mucklow
Copyeditor: Phyllis Mueller
Graphics: Dianne Miller, KRT Graphics, Inc.
Styling: Susan E. Mickey and Roger Foster
Administration: Jim Baskett

Library of Congress Cataloging-in-Publication Data

Mickey, Susan E.
  Sewing projects in an afternoon / Susan E. Mickey.
     p. cm.
  Includes index.
  ISBN 1-4027-0644-8
  1. Machine sewing. I. Title.
TT713 .M53 2003
646.2--dc22

                                                              2003017485

10 9 8 7 6 5 4 3 2 1

Published in paperback in 2005 by Sterling Publishing Co., Inc.
387 Park Avenue South, New York, N.Y. 10016

© 2004 by Prolific Impressions, Inc.

Produced by Prolific Impressions, Inc.
160 South Candler St., Decatur, GA 30030

Distributed in Canada by Sterling Publishing
c/o Canadian Manda Group, 165 Dufferin Street
Toronto, Ontario, Canada M6K 3H6
Distributed in Great Britain by Chrysalis Books Group PLC
The Chrysalis Building, Bramley Road, London W10 6SP, England
Distributed in Australia by Capricorn Link (Australia) Pty. Ltd.
P.O. Box 704, Windsor, NSW 2756 Australia
Printed in China
All rights reserved
Sterling ISBN 1-4027-0644-8 Hardcover
        ISBN 1-4027-2238-9 Paperback

About Susan E. Mickey

Susan E. Mickey is an accomplished designer with over 20 years experience. As a costume designer, she is particularly known for her interpretations of period clothing for stage and film. Susan is also an experienced photo stylist with thousands of photographs for books, magazines, and catalogs to her credit. She lives on a sheep farm near Atlanta, Georgia with her husband, sculptor Roger Foster.

Acknowledgments

Thank you, **Carol Hammond**, for helping me coordinate and develop the projects in this book. Thank you, **Carol Sadler**, for being the fastest and most steadfast stitcher I know – you are an inspiration with your sewing machine! Thank you to my sweet **Grandmother Waggoner**, who taught me all of the stitching there is to be done by hand. My everlasting gratitude is reserved for my dear mother, **Mary Mickey**, my first sewing inspiration, who initially sat me down at a sewing machine and proceeded to persevere through my impatience and tears.

sewing se

ng   sewing

If you have a few hours, you can make the projects in this book. You may wish to surprise someone with a hand-made present or just create your own style by choosing and combining fabrics and colors that can't be found in stores. Whether your motivation is saving money or expressing your creativity, these projects will guide you through a rewarding afternoon of sewing. Most of the designs in this book are simple enough for the beginning needlecraft enthusiast; each project is labeled beginner, intermediate, or advanced for easy reference.

Be a stitcher

Sewing is a skill that everyone thought was necessary for survival just two generations ago, but now it is rare that a young person even knows how to thread a needle.

This book includes basic information you need to know in order to sew almost anything. A person who creates with her (or his) own hands achieves well-being and gains the ability to view the beauty around them with deeper appreciation.

Sewing can be a therapeutic and relaxing activity. If you already know how to sew, teach someone else. They will always remember you, and they will own a valuable skill for life.

From the Author

As a costume designer, I am always surrounded by beautiful fabrics, stacks of colorful thread, boxes of trim, and bins of ribbon. Buttons are usually stored in big metal filing cabinets, and notions are always at the ready and displayed on shelves. Packs of bias trim and little boxes of safety pins in all sizes are lined up like soldiers waiting to be called to duty. This is the world where I work and spend most of my time. I feel lucky. Although costume shops are not always glamorous, their inhabitants are some of the most interesting people you will ever meet. They are professionals who sew for a living and love it. The drapers make the patterns, and the first hands cut the fabric and stitch the patterns together. In costume shops throughout the country, where costumes and garments of all periods and shapes are made for the entertainment industry, the people who work all day long at sewing machines are called stitchers.

Stitching is a noble profession, but it is increasingly difficult to find young people who have either the skills or the will to enter this profession. Historically a female profession, stitching is now an equal opportunity field, and just as some great chefs are men, so too are some of the most talented sewing artisans.

The projects in this book were made and the instructions tested by the Costume Shop at the Alliance Theatre in Atlanta, Georgia where I have spent a great deal of time during my career. The names of the fine craft artisans who created the projects are listed on each project.

I hope you enjoy this book.

Sincerely,

Susan E. Mickey

Proper Tools for Sewing

Sewing Machine & Accessories

Your **sewing machine** needs to have straight-stitch, zigzag, and buttonhole capabilities. A good machine will not make you a better stitcher, but a good machine can make things go smoothly and keep a beginner from getting too frustrated. I asked all of the people who participated in this book about the machines they use and what they recommend. They told me they prefer a machine with metal parts – a simple machine without fancy stitches. The stitch on your machine should be smooth and beautiful. There are some really fancy machines on the market, and a good machine can set you back big bucks. But there are always used machines that are terrific deals at yard sales, in shops that sell new sewing machines, and in the newspaper. If you are a beginner, pal up with a sewing buddy who knows the ropes. Ask them to look at the machine you're considering before you take the plunge. I recommend you purchase something inexpensive at first and then move on to a machine with more sophistication and glide when you become smitten with the craft.

A **serger** or **overlock machine** that makes a professionally finished edge is a great new invention in home sewing. It is not always necessary, but is fun and useful to own, nonetheless.

Using good quality **thread**, which doesn't break or tangle easily, keeps frustration and cursing to a minimum. Thread has a shelf life, so beware – if you raid old Aunt Cynthia's stash of spools from the 30s the thread will probably be rotten or weak.

Different **needles** do different things. You always need to use the appropriate needle for the weight of fabric you are using and the kind of stitch you want to make. This goes for hand-sewing needles as well as machine needles. Thin, fine needles are for lighter weight fabrics; heavier, larger needles are for heavier weight fabrics. Ball point needles are for knits and fabrics that you don't want to puncture when sewing.

Iron

A really good iron is *most* important – choose one with strong steaming and pressing capabilities. Often the difference between something that looks homemade and something that has a professional finish can be measured in the pressing of each step. Buy as nice and heavy duty an iron as you can afford. You will never regret it.

The sturdier your **ironing board**, the better. It should be large enough to easily press your project. You can make an ironing table with a little batting and muslin if you have room to keep something like that around. Otherwise, a collapsible one that folds away for storage is just fine.

Scissors

The single most important tool you will own is your scissors. Spare no expense! Use **fabric scissors** specially made for the job of cutting fabric. When you go to buy a scissors, hold it in your hand so that you can be sure the size and weight are right for you. Do not let *anyone* else use your scissors – cutting through something metal (even a pin!) can ruin a good pair. Constant thread clipping can dull a good pair of scissors, as can using them to cut paper or other non-fabric items.

So in your cutting arsenal, you also need a little pair of **snipping scissors** to keep at the machine just for thread clipping, and a pair of **craft/paper scissors** for cutting out patterns and other non-fabric items. These can be inexpensive, and you can replace them often. I also like to keep a pair of **tailor's points** on hand. They are small, very sharp, and ideal for clipping curves and corners. Use **pinking shears** for cutting fabrics that may ravel badly and for cutting decorative edges.

Pattern Measuring & Marking

- A 36" **wooden yardstick** is invaluable. Professionals use an 18" (or longer) **clear plastic ruler** for marking patterns.
- A **compass** will come in handy for drawing circles and curves.
- I like **straight pins** with ball heads – everyone has a personal preference, but I think they are easier on your fingers.
- I prefer **brown kraft paper** for pattern making. It is sturdy and holds up with repeated use.
- For marking, you will need **tailor's chalk** – blue for light fabrics, white for dark. A **disappearing marker** for marking patterns is always handy and provides an easy way to mark lines that later can be steamed or ironed away.
- A flexible **measuring tape** is needed for measuring yourself and your loved ones and instilling fear in people who lack self-confidence about their bodies. (It's true! Wear it around your neck and ask people if you can measure their waist. For every person who makes an excuse ("I'm bloated," "I just ate," "I just went through the holidays"), you can send me a nickel.)

Other Tools & Supplies

- Hopefully, you will never need a **seam ripper**, but buy one anyway. (I use mine constantly.) I also use a **craft knife** for un-doing seams and for cutting buttonholes.
- For keeping unfinished edges from raveling away, you will need a small bottle of **liquid fabric sealer**.
- Though it may feel awkward at first, using a **thimble** will make all your handwork go faster and will keep the needle's head from poking a hole in your finger. (Ouch!) I am addicted to using a thimble and cannot hand-sew without one.
- For turning a spaghetti strap or any other long, thin strip, you need a **loop turner**. I have substituted chopsticks and other inappropriate pokey things, but if you turn things frequently, invest in turning tubes. Find them in specialty sewing catalogs and large sewing stores. They are faster, less frustrating, and worth it!
- A **point turner** is used for pushing out points from the inside of a project. It has a blunt point so it won't poke a hole in your fabric (like the points of your scissors can).

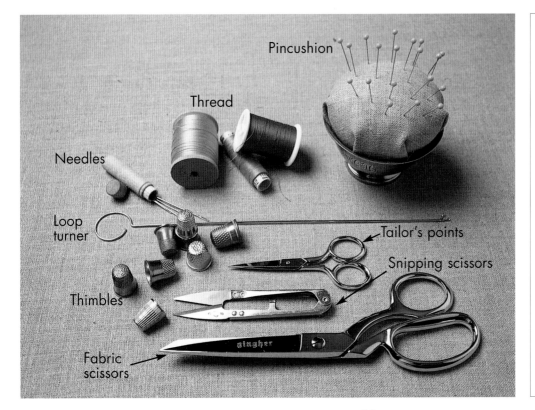

Pincushion
Thread
Needles
Loop turner
Thimbles
Fabric scissors
Tailor's points
Snipping scissors

See Appendix on pages 116-125 for a glossary of terms and explanation of techniques

Fabrics for Sewing

Fabric is right next to food (and for me, dishes) as one of life's great joys. I find it almost impossible to walk into a fabric store and not feel my way through the aisles. Fabric choice is an important element of the success or failure of your sewing effort.

Although we wear fabric every day, we may not consider what it's made of or how it's made. Knowing a little bit about fabrics will keep you from frustration and anguish later.

Fabric can be yarn-dyed (the yarn is dyed before it is woven or knitted) or piece dyed (the fabric is dyed after it is woven or knitted). Fabric can be printed with patterns on the surface or dyed with a technique like tie-dyeing or batik.

The Big Categories

natural fibers

wool   flax
silk   linen
cotton

man-made fibers

acetate   polyester
acrylic   rayon
fleece   spandex
metallics   tencel
microfibers   tri-acetate
nylon   interfacing

About Fiber

All fabric is composed of fiber. Fiber can be **natural** or **man-made**, and woven, knitted, or fused. A basic knowledge of fiber categories will help you choose fabrics wisely. It will also help you care for clothing and table linens – you will be able to understand the fiber content and care labels and learn exactly how garments will wear and behave.

About weave

Now that you have an idea of what the individual fibers are (see box on page 12), let's make them into whole cloth.

Fabric is either woven, knitted, or fused. When we say a fabric is cotton, we are identifying the **fiber**. When we say it is twill, we are identifying the **weave**. A fabric may be woven of many different types of fiber; for instance, satin (the weave) may be made of polyester, wool, or silk (the fiber). It may seem confusing, but it is really very simple.

Satin Weave

is characterized by its luxurious shine and surface sheen.

Pile Weaves

are characterized by their soft, thick, fuzzy surfaces.

Pile weaves not pictured but commonly used are terry cloth, which is usually of natural cotton fiber; and fleece which is a synthetic finber.

Plain weave or tabby

is characterized by threads that run alternately over the other.

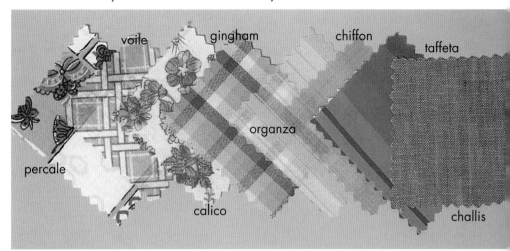

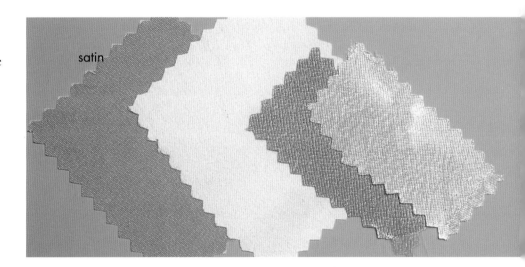

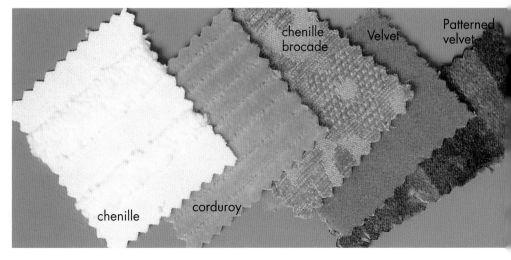

Twill Weave

is characterized by a diagonal ridge running through the weave on the fabric surface.

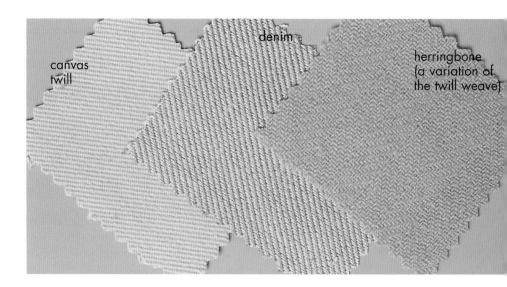

Pattern Weaves

are characterized by a subtle or elaborate design in the surface of the fabric that is intrinsic to the weave, not stamped or printed on the surface.

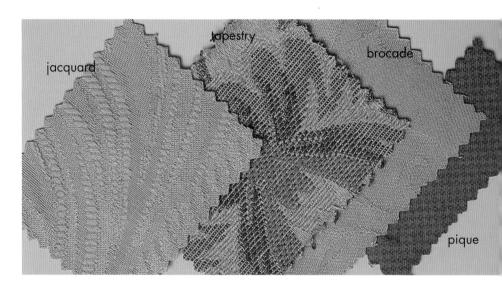

Knit

is characterized by interlocking loops of fiber. There are many types of knits, but suffice it to say that they behave differently from woven fabrics. They will have a slight to extreme *stretch* (usually), and ravel differently than woven fabrics when cut.

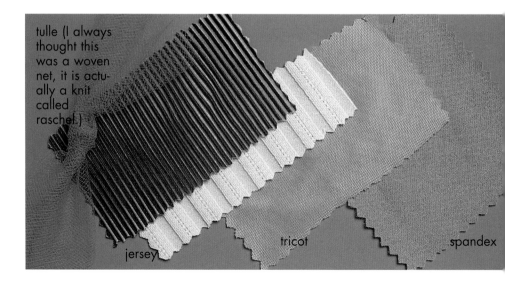

Netting

is characterized by an intricate knotting and lacing of threads.

lace

Felt

is fused, matted loose fiber. As there are no individual yarns to ravel, you may cut felt and not worry about finishing the edge.

Bonded Fabrics

are two fabrics fused together with a fiber adhesive agent.

industrial felt

wool felt

craft felt (usually a combination of synthetic mystery fibers and, like a hot dog, you probably don't want to know what it's made of)

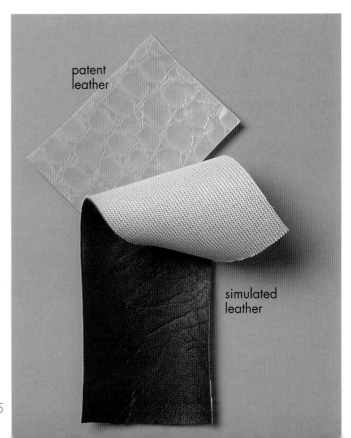

patent leather

simulated leather

Pillows

Pillows are a simple way to change a color scheme or enhance a theme in a room of your home. The envelope pillow and pillow slipcover show how to make a cover for an existing pillow or pillow form that can be removed for easy cleaning. Colorful pillows also can be made quickly from vintage hankies or decorator napkins you may already own. The tooth fairy pillow is especially easy and makes a unique gift.

Fabrics Recommended

silk dupioni
wool
brocade
jacquard
linen
cotton
canvas

Level of Ability

beginner

Envelope Pillow

by Jennifer Jacob

This pillow closes with a flap, like an envelope does. The flap can be triangular, rectangular, semicircular, or a freehand shape you draw – just be sure the top edge of the flap is the same length as the top edge of the pillow. A button is used to hold the flap closed. Make your own pattern for this pillow.

1. The cut fabric pieces for the pillow.

fabric and notions needed:

■ Pillow form or old pillow
■ 1/2-1 yd. fabric (how much you need depends on the size of your pillow)
■ Button
■ Thread

make a pattern

1. Measure your pillow. Add 1-1/2" to these dimensions for seam allowances and ease. *Example: Your pillow measures 18" x 18". Your pattern will be 19-1/2" x 19-1/2".*
2. Either make a pattern or simply mark the fabric for cutting.
3. Design a flap and mark on fabric or make a pattern. Use the photo as an example of the shape. Be sure the top edge of the flap is the same width as the pillow fabric dimension. *Example: the top edge of the flap would measure 19-1/2".* **Note:** If your flap is NOT rectangular but a triangle as shown, add 1-1/2" (with straight sides, like the pillow) at the top of the flap so the flap will lay nicely. [**photo 1**]

2. Stitching the front to the back.

cut the fabric

1. Cut two pieces (front and back) to your pattern dimensions.
2. Cut a third piece of fabric for the flap.
3. Cut a lining for the flap that is the same size and shape as the flap.

3. Attaching the flap.

stitch it up

1. Place the flap and flap lining with right sides together. Stitch, using a 1/2" seam allowance around all sides of the flap, leaving the top edge open. Trim seams. Turn the flap right side out. Press flat.
2. Turn under the top edge of the pillow front 1/2" and hem.
3. With right sides together, using 1/2" seam allowance, stitch front and back pieces together around the sides and bottom. [**photo 2**] Clip corners to reduce bulk. Turn right side out and press flat.
4. With right sides together, using a 1/2" seam allowance, stitch the top edge of the flap to the top edge of the back. Press the seam allowance towards the flap. Fold the raw edge of the lining of the flap in 1/2" and pin. Stitch in the ditch to secure and finish flap. [**photo 3**]

5. For a button closure, mark and sew buttonhole(s) on the flap. Sew the button(s) in corresponding place(s) on the front. ❑

Variations

• Use the design on the fabric as the shape of the edge of the flap.

• Add tassels, ruffles, or fringe to the edges of the flap.

• Pipe the pillow and/or the flap with bias covered cording.

• Use ties instead of a button to secure the flap. Insert the ties in the flap seam and the bottom seam of the pillow before sewing, placing them so they will match up.

Napkin or Hankie Pillow

by Carol Hammond

A quick and easy pillow can be made with a pair of napkins or hand-kerchiefs. The finished edges of the napkin or handkerchief are visible and so become an important part of the design.

fabric and notions needed:

▓ 2 Cloth napkins the same size *or* 2 vintage hankies the same (or near the same) size

▓ Pillow form or stuffing

▓ Thread

Pictured below: A napkin pillow

stitch it up

1. Pin both napkins/hankies with *wrong* sides together, leaving a 4" opening at the top.
2. Topstitch the napkins or hankies together close to the edge, leaving the 4" opening.
3. Stuff the pillow through the opening.
4. Stitch the remaining 4" to close. ❏

Variations

• Sew a button at the center of each pillow.

• Trim with fringe, tassels, or other items.

• Bead over a design. See the appendix for instructions.

• Combine any of these variations.

Pictured at right: hankie pillows

Pillow Slipcover

by Jennifer Jacob

Insert the pillow form through the opening on the back – no zipper needed! What could be easier?

fabric and notions needed:

▪ 1/2 to 1 yd. fabric (depending on the size of the pillow)
▪ Pillow form
▪ Thread

make a pattern

1. Measure your pillow form. Add 1-1/2" to these dimensions for seam allowances and ease.
2. Make a pattern or mark directly on the fabric.

cut your fabrics

1. Cut one front piece to the pattern dimensions.
2. Cut two back pieces that are half of the pattern width plus 2" and the full height of the pattern. *Example:* To make a 14" square pillow, cut one front piece that measures 15-1/2" x 15-1/2" and two back pieces that measure 15-1/2" x 9-3/4".

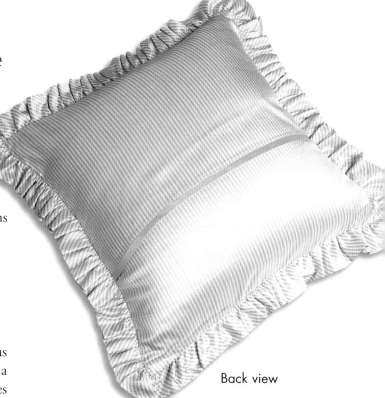

Back view

stitch it up

1. Make a rolled hem or bind one horizontal side of each back piece. (For binding instructions, see the appendix.)
2. Overlap the two finished edges of the back pieces to make one back piece that is the same size as the front piece. With right sides facing up, stitch around the edges to hold the pieces in place.
3. With right sides together, stitch the front piece to the back pieces around all sides, using a 1/2" seam allowance.
4. Press your seams open. Trim or clip corners.
5. Turn right side out. Press flat.
6. Insert the pillow form. ❏

Variations

• Add buttons and buttonholes to the overlap.

• Add piping, fringe, or a ruffle to the seam.

• Applique or bead a motif on the front.

• Add fringed or beaded tassels to the corners.

• Color block or piece your panels with different fabrics.

Tooth Fairy Pillow

by Jennifer Jacob

This tiny pillow is a wonderful gift for a child – a pocket holds first the tooth, then the gift of the fairy. The pieced top requires very little fabric.

fabric and notions needed:

- 1/4 yd. each of two contrasting fabrics *or* scraps
- 3/4 yd. lace, 1/2" to 3/4" wide
- Pillow stuffing
- Thread to match fabric
- Chalk
- *optional:* small shank button

Fig. 1

cut

cut

6" square fabric 1 pillow bottom

6" square fabric 2 pillow top

Fig. 2

attach triangles to square

fabric 1

fold

4" square fabric 1 pillow top

4" square fabric 2 pocket

cut your fabrics

See Fig. 1.

1. Cut a 6" square (pillow bottom) and a 4" square (pillow top) from fabric #1.
2. Cut a 6" square from fabric #2 (triangles on pillow top).
3. Using chalk, draw diagonal lines from opposite corners to divide the 6" square from fabric #2 into four triangles. Cut on the chalked lines.
4. Cut a 4" square from fabric #2 for the pocket.

stitch it up

1. Fold the 4" pocket square into a triangle and press. Set aside.
2. With right sides together, using 1/4" seam allowance, stitch the long edges of two triangles to opposite sides of the 4" square of fabric #1. Press seam allowances toward the triangles. [**photo 1**] *See Fig. 2.*
3. With right sides together, using a 1/4" seam allowance, stitch the remaining two triangles to the remaining sides of the square, stitching across other triangle to end of pieces. Press seam allowances toward the triangles.

4. Place the pressed pocket triangle over the right side of one triangle on the pieced block. Line up the folded edge of the pocket with the seam of the triangle of the center square. Stitch the two unhemmed edges to secure. [**photo 2**] This piece is the pillow top. True it back into a square, if necessary, by pressing and trimming. (Be sure to leave a 1/4" seam allowance.)
5. Pin the lace along the stitching line on the right side of the trued top with the finished lace edge to the inside.
6. Stack the top and bottom with right sides together. (The bottom may be slightly bigger than your trued top. If it is, trim it to match for easier sewing.) Using a 1/4" seam allowance, stitch the top to the bottom catching the lace between the layers [**photo 3**]. Leave a 1" opening at the top for turning.
7. Trim corners and seams.
8. Turn pillow right side out and stuff until firm.
9. Slipstitch opening closed.
10. *Option:* With a hand needle and a double strand of thread, stitch through the center of pillow and add a button. ❏

sew with your children
sew for yourself
make a little something
with that fabric on the shelf

1. Pressing the triangles after stitching.

2. Stitching the pocket over one corner.

3. Sewing the seam with lace inserted.

Blanket Throw

This project is made with a purchased twin bed blanket cut in half. These blankets can be found at home, discount, and department stores – one inexpensive blanket will make two beautiful throws for napping. Choose a contrasting fabric for the binding that accents your room and expresses your style.

A bound throw makes a personal, elegant wedding or birthday gift. You may find yourself scavenging the closeout bins for cotton blankets and collecting fabulous fabrics for binding.

Fabrics Recommended for Binding

silk dupioni
cotton calico, gingham
wool
organza

Level of Ability

beginner

Sewing can be a therapeutic and relaxing activity. Someone who creates with their own hands achieves well being and gains an ability to view the world with deeper appreciation.

Blanket Throw

fabric and notions needed:

- 1 cotton twin-size blanket, 66" x 90" (purchased)
- 1 yd. fashion fabric
- Thread to match fashion fabric
- Chalk

cut your fabrics

1. Cut the 90" side of blanket in half so each piece measures 66" x 45".
2. Cut away all of the remaining factory finished seam allowances so that all of the edges are raw (to avoid lumpiness). Straighten any edges.
3. Straighten the fashion fabric. (See the "bias" section of the appendix for instructions.) Press.
4. Make 7 yards of 8" wide bias strips of fashion fabric (See the "bias" section of the appendix.) Fold bias strips in half lengthwise and baste together along the raw edge.

stitch it up

1. Draw a line 3/8" from the raw edge of the bias to mark the seam allowance.
2. On the wrong side of the blanket, draw a line 1-1/2" from the raw edges. [photo 1]
3. With right sides together, baste the bias strip to the blanket, mitering the corners. [photo 2] (See the appendix for information about mitering corners.)
4. Machine stitch along the basting and mitered corners.
5. Press.
6. Fold the bias binding over the edge of throw to the wrong side and pin. [photo 3] Finish, using a blindstitch, mitering the corners. ❏

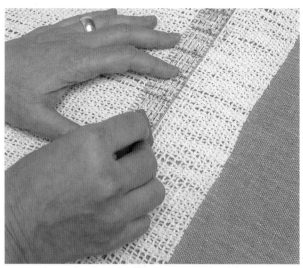
1. Marking the seam allowance on the blanket.

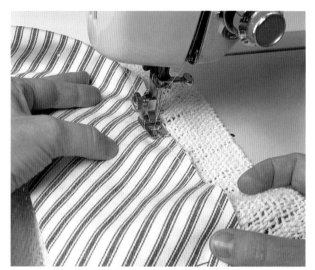
2. Basting the binding to the blanket.

3. The binding pinned in place.

Teapot Cozy

by Renee Holland

This clever cozy keeps the teapot warm so you can enjoy a second cup. It's an ideal gift for your tea-loving friends or a special treat you can make for yourself.

This design can easily be converted, with the addition of a few pockets and some elastic loops, into an elegant bag for travel toiletries.

Fabrics Recommended

cotton
quilted cotton
silk shantung
canvas

Level of Ability

intermediate

"Sewing makes me feel like
an individual, while
connecting me with my past
and my family."

Renee Holland

Teapot Cozy

fabric and notions needed:

- 1/3 yd. fashion fabric
- 2/3 yd. contrasting fabric
- 1/2 yd. cotton flannel
- 2 buttons, 7/8"
- 2 yds. ribbon *or* 2 yds. bias-covered cord made from the fashion or other fabric *or* purchased cord
- Thread
- Disappearing marker
- Brown paper for pattern making

Special note: Marks on the right side of the fabric should be made with a disappearing marker – the kind that is easily removed with steam or water. Test any marking tool on your fabric before using.

make a pattern

1. Draw a 7" x 12" rectangle on kraft paper for the flap.
2. With craft scissors, cut to round off two corners as shown in diagram. *To round off the corners, I find it easier to fold the fabric in half and cut through two layers, rounding the corners. this way you have matching corners.* [photo 1]

cut your fabrics

See Fig. 1.

1. From fashion fabric, cut four pieces for the flaps, using your paper pattern.
2. From flannel, cut two flaps, using your paper pattern.
3. From flannel, cut one 15" x 12" rectangle for insulation.
4. From contrasting fabric, cut two 15" x 12" rectangles for the body of cozy.

stitch it up

Construct the body piece:

1. Stack the two rectangular pieces with right sides together. Lay the flannel rectangle on top.
2. Stitch around the edge, using a 1/2" seam allowance. Leave a 2" opening on one edge for turning. [photo 2] Clip corners and trim seams. Turn. Press flat. The flannel will be inside the front and back pieces and act as an insulator.
3. Mark 2" squares for quilting on body and topstitch along the quilting lines.

Construct the flaps:

4. Stack two flap pieces of fashion fabric with right sides together. Lay one flannel piece on top.
5. Stitch around the two short sides and along the curved bottom of flap, using a 1/2" seam allowance. [photo 3]
6. Repeat for second flap.
7. Trim and clip the seams. Turn flaps and press. The flannel will be sandwiched between the fashion fabric pieces, and will act as insulation.
8. At top of flap, turn raw edges to the inside. Topstitch 1/8" from edge along top and along all sides of both flaps.
9. Mark lines for quilting on both flaps. Topstitch on the quilting lines. [photo 4]

Assemble:

10. Divide the long side of the body in thirds and mark horizontal lines from one side to the other. (These are your fold lines.) Topstitch the lines. *See Fig. 2.* [photo 5]
11. On the back of each flap, measure 3-1/2" down from the top of flap and mark a line.
12. Lay each flap face down and line up the 12" side of the body piece along the marked lines on the flaps. Pin to hold. *See Fig. 3.*

1. Making the pattern for the flap.

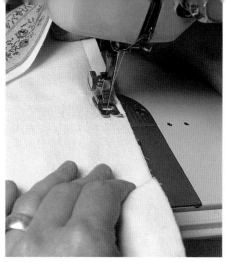

2. Stitching the bottom.

3. Stitching a flap.

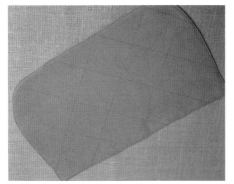

4. A quilted flap.

5. Stitching the fold lines on the bottom piece.

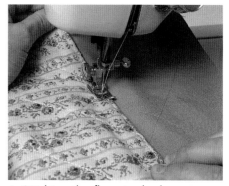

6. Stitching the flaps to the bottom piece.

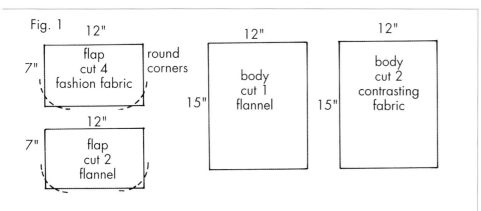

Fig. 1

12"
7" flap cut 4 fashion fabric | round corners

12"
7" flap cut 2 flannel

12"
15" body cut 1 flannel

12"
15" body cut 2 contrasting fabric

Fig. 2

topstitch
- - - -
topstitch

Fig. 3

flap
body
backside

13. Turn to right side and topstitch along the curved edges of the flaps through all thicknesses 1/8" from the edge of the flap. [**photo 6**]

14. Topstitch a tie at the center top of each flap and halfway down the sides of each flap.

15. Sew a decorative button at the bottom center of each flap.

NOTE: For more thorough instructions on quilting any project, please see the appendix. ❏

Travel Toiletry Bag

This luxurious-looking travel bag is simple to make but carries lots of style. It is made in the same way as the tea cozy with a slight variation.

Fabrics Recommended

cotton

quilted cotton

silk shantung

canvas

brocade

Level of Ability

intermediate

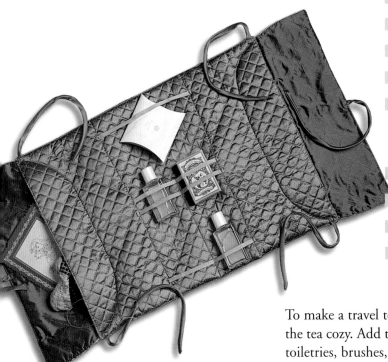

fabric and notions needed:

- 1/3 yd. fashion fabric
- 2/3 yd. contrasting fabric
- 1/2 yd. cotton flannel
- 2 buttons, 7/8"
- 2 yds. ribbon *or* 2 yds. bias-covered cord made from the fashion or other fabric *or* purchased cord
- Thread
- Elastic tape or additional fabric for pockets
- Disappearing marker
- Kraft paper

To make a travel toiletries bag, cut and assemble all pieces just the same as for the tea cozy. Add the inside pockets and/or elastic straps for holding travel-size toiletries, brushes, etc. to the body piece before assembling.

An extra personal touch would be to applique or monogram the outside flap. ❑

Chair Covers by Renee Holland

Here's an idea for sprucing up your old wicker furniture and adding a little color to your porch or patio.

Fabrics Recommended

cotton

canvas

anything with a little body to it that's completely washable

Level of Ability

beginner

Chair Covers

The instructions below tell you how to make the cover for the chair back. Purchase additional fabric and piping to make a cushion for the chair seat, using one of the pillow project instructions in this book. For more information on bias binding and making bias strips, see the appendix.

fabrics and notions needed:

For one chair cover:

- 1/2 yd. fashion fabric
- 1/2 yd. contrasting fabric (for binding, back, and ties)
- Piping (For instructions for making piping, see the appendix.)

make a pattern

Our chair measured 29" across at a point about 17" down from the center back. Your chair measurements may vary.

1. Measure your chair. Add 1-1/2" all the way around your chair measurements for ease and seam allowance.
2. Make a pattern by drawing a semicircle to your new dimensions. [**photo 1**]

cut your fabrics

1. Cut one front from the fashion fabric, one back from the contrast fabric, and enough 4" wide bias strips to go around the whole chair back.
2. Cut two 4" x 36" bias strips of contrast fabric for the ties.

stitch it up

1. Fold the bias strips for the ties in half lengthwise and stitch one short end and the long side. Turn. Press. Position the ties, with the raw end aligned with the seam allowance, 4" up from the bottom of the back cover and baste them in place. [**photo 2**]
2. Stitch the piping on the right side of the front piece along the stitching line with the piping facing *towards* the center of the piece.
3. With right sides together, stitch the front and back pieces together around the curved top, using a 1/2" seam allowance.

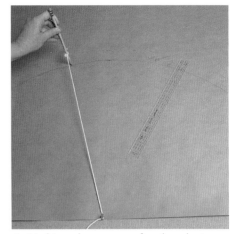

1. Making the pattern for the chair back.

2. Machine-basting the ties in place.

3. Stitching the bias binding to the bottom edge.

4. Clip around the curved seam. Turn to the right side and press.

5. Apply the bias binding to the bottom edge of the cover all the way around. [**photo 3**] Make sure you begin and end on the back, but stitch neatly so the cover can be reversible. ❑

Variation

• Use pieces of vintage tablecloths or old quilts to make the chair covers.

Duvet Cover

by Cindy Lou Who

This washable, changeable duvet cover was made with purchased sheets. If you can catch a sale on great flat sheets, you can combine them with some trim fabric for a custom look. Make the front and the back from different colors or patterns and you will have a reversible bed cover for different seasons.

Fabrics Recommended

cotton
washable brocade
linen

Level of Ability

advanced

Duvet Cover

fabric and notions needed:

- 2 flat queen sheets, each 102" x 90"
- 9 buttons
- Thread
- 2-1/2 yds. fashion fabric
- 2-1/2 yds. contrast fabric

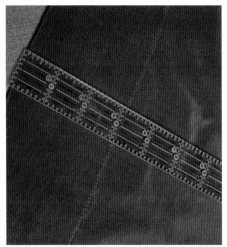

1. Topstitching the hem on the long edge of the fashion fabric.

2. Seaming the fashion and contrast fabrics.

cut your fabrics

See Fig. 1.

1. On the sheet that will be the top of the duvet cover, cut a 23" strip off the bottom.
2. On the sheet that will become the bottom of the duvet cover, cut a 6" strip off the bottom.
3. Cut a 20" wide strip of fashion fabric 92" long.
4. Cut a 17-1/2" wide strip of contrast fabric 92" long.

stitch it up

1. With right sides together, stitch the long sides of the contrast fabric and fashion fabric, using a 1/2" seam allowance. Trim and finish the seams with either a zigzag stitch or an overlocked edge.
2. Turn under a scant 1/2" on the sides of the fashion fabric/contrast fabric piece. *See Fig. 2.* Top stitch.
3. To begin to make the button hole flap, turn under the long edge of the fashion fabric 3". Press. Pin this 3" in place to hold. Turn this hem back to front side and stitch a side seam along this 3" hem. Turn this hem right side out. Topstitch along the pressed long edge. [**photo 1**]

4. Mark the buttonholes across the top edge of the fashion fabric, spacing them evenly and leaving 2" on each side for the seams. *Tip:* Test the spacing with pins. The start of the buttonhole should be 1/8" + half the width of the button. For example, a buttonhole for a 1" button would start 5/8" away from the folded edge.
5. Make the buttonholes. (The three layers of fabric will stabilize the buttonholes.)
6. With right sides together, stitch the fashion and contrast fabrics to the top of the back sheet, using a 1/2" seam allowance. [**photo 2**] *See Fig. 3.*
7. With the right sides together. Stitch the front and back sheets together along the bottom edge, using a 1/2" seam allowance.
8. With right sides together, stitch the sides of the front and back, using a 1/2" seam allowance. (The back of the duvet cover is longer than the front to allow for the buttoned foldover.) Turn right side out.
9. On the sides of the added piece (fashion fabric/contrast fabric piece), turn under 1/2" hem so that edges of this piece are even with the edge of the back sheet piece. Top stitch.
10. Mark the placement of the buttons to match up with the buttonholes. Sew the buttons by hand. ❑

Fig. 1

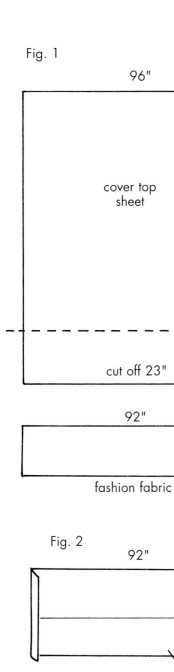

96"

cover top
sheet

cut off 23"

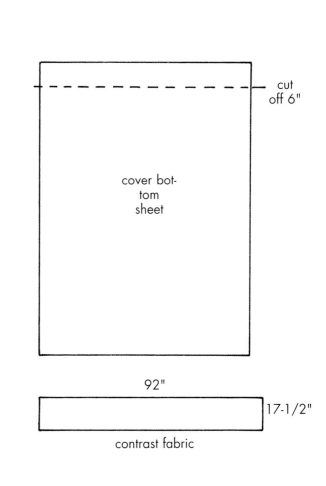

cut
off 6"

cover bot-
tom
sheet

92"

20"

fashion fabric

92"

17-1/2"

contrast fabric

Fig. 2

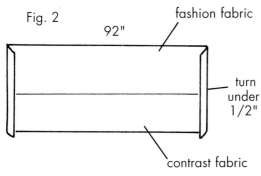

fashion fabric

92"

turn
under
1/2"

contrast fabric

Fig. 3

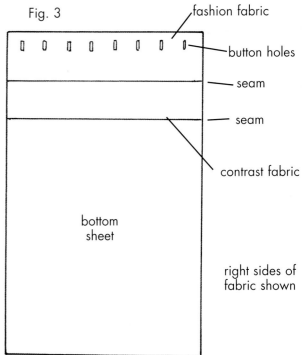

fashion fabric

button holes

seam

seam

contrast fabric

bottom
sheet

right sides of
fabric shown

Napkins • Placemats • Coasters

A wonderful way to start sewing is by making something simple for your home, and these are some of the simplest projects in this book. The coasters, especially, are useful for a special cocktail party, and they make a thoughtful hostess gift. Placemats and napkins in unique fabrics can be a keepsake wedding present.

Fabrics Recommended

fine linen damask

cotton

brocades

silk (this may limit the washability so use caution)

quilted cotton (for placemats and coasters)

Level of Ability

beginner

Reversible Placemats

by Cindy Lou Who

The instructions that follow are for one placemat. You may need to adjust the measurements for unique or unusual table settings or smaller than average tables. For more thorough instructions for bias binding, see the appendix. You can use quilted cotton that is finished on both sides, or use quilted fabric on one side and regular fabric for reverse side.

fabric and notions needed:

for four placemats:

- 1 yd. fabric (for the fronts)
- 1 yd. contrasting fabric (for the backs)
- 1 yd. accent fabric (for binding)
- Thread
- Brown paper for pattern making

make a pattern

Make a rectangular kraft paper pattern 18" x 13". This is the size of the finished placemat – you will not lose any of the size to seam allowances.

cut your fabrics

1. Cut one rectangle from the fashion fabric and one from the contrasting fabric. If you are using reversible quilted cotton, you will need to cut one rectangle per placemat.
2. Cut the accent fabric into 2" wide bias strips, enough to make 65" of bias binding.

stitch it up

1. With *wrong* sides together, pin or baste the front to the back. [**photo 1**] *Not necessary if you are using reversible quilted fabric.*
2. Press the bias binding in half.
3. Bind the edge of the placemat with bias binding and finish. [**photo 2**] ❏

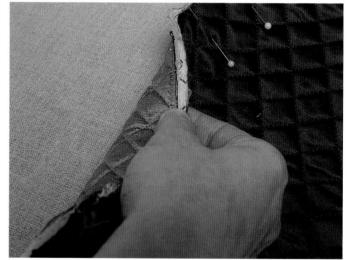

1. Pin basting the two fabrics, wrong sides together.

2. Binding the edge.

Octagon Placemat Variation

make a pattern

1. Starting with the basic rectangular paper pattern, measure 2" in from every corner and mark. Across every corner, connect the two marks on each side to create triangles. [**photo 3**]
2. Cut off the triangles of the four points.

Follow the instructions for cutting and stitching given for the Reversible Placemat.

Wedge Placemat Variation

Wedge-shaped placemats work well on round tables.

make a pattern

1. Starting with the basic rectangular paper pattern, fold the pattern piece in half crosswise (13" to 13" touching) to create a center crease. Unfold to reveal the crease.
2. At the top, mark 5" from the center crease on each side.
3. Draw from that mark to the bottom corner of the corresponding side. [**photo 4**]
4. Cut off the corners.

Follow the instructions for cutting and stitching given for the Reversible Placemat.

3. Marking the corner triangles to create the octagon variation and oval variation placemats.

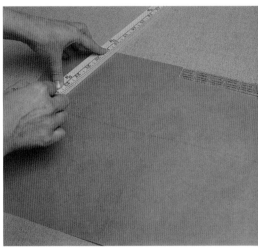

4. Marking the pattern to create the wedge variation placemat.

Oval Placemat Variation

make a pattern

1. Starting with the basic rectangular paper pattern, measure 2" in from every corner and mark. Across every corner, connect the two marks on each side to create triangles. [**photo 3**]
2. Cut off the triangles of the four points. Round all of the edges to create an oval shape.

Follow the instructions for cutting and stitching given for the Reversible Placemat.

Cocktail Napkins

by Renee Holland

fabric and notions needed:

- 2 yds. fabric
- Thread

cut your fabric

Cut four 14" squares of fabric.

stitch it up

1. On all four sides, fold down a 1/2" hem to the wrong side. Press.
2. Fold under 1/2" again. Press.
3. Unfold fabric. Trim across each corner to make a miter. [photo 1]
4. Fold the first 1/2" hem down again to the wrong side.
5. At the corners of the napkin, place right sides of the hem together and stitch across the corners at a 45 degree angle to the edge of the fabric. [photo 2] Trim off the extra fabric at the corner triangles and press the seams open.
6. Turn the second hem under 1/2" on the wrong side of the fabric, and press.
7. Edgestitch the hem around the napkin. [photo 3] ❑

1. The double hems are pressed and the mitered corner is trimmed.

2. Stitching the mitered corner.

3. Edgestitching the hem.

Variations

- For a dinner napkin, make a 1" deep hem on a 22" square.

- Make a picot edge on napkins by using a narrow and short zigzag stitch to overcast the edge, stitching just on and off the edge of the fabric.

- Applique or embroider a design on one corner of the napkin.

47

Coasters

by Cindy Lou Who and Renee Holland

Quilted fabrics are a good choice for coasters.

Round Coasters

fabrics and notions needed:

- 1/8 yd. fashion fabric
- 1/8 yd. contrast fabric
- Accent fabric
- Thread
- Brown paper for pattern making

make a pattern

From kraft paper, cut a 4" diameter circle for the pattern.

cut your fabrics

1. Cut one circle of the fashion fabric and one of the contrast fabric.
2. Cut enough accent fabric to make a 2" wide, 16" long bias strip for binding.

stitch it up

1. With wrong sides together, pin or baste the fashion fabric to the contrast fabric.
2. Fold the bias strip in half and press.
3. Bind the edges with bias binding and stitch to finish. [photo] ❑

Finishing the edge of a round coaster with bias binding.

Square Coasters

fabric and notions needed:

- 1/8 yd. fashion fabric
- 1/8 yd. fashion fabric
- Thread
- Kraft paper

make a pattern

From kraft paper, make a 5" square pattern.

cut your fabrics

1. Cut one square from the fashion fabric.
2. Cut one square from the contrast fabric.

stitch it up

1. With right sides together, stitch around three sides with a 1/8" seam allowance.
2. Clip corners
3. Turn right side out and press, pressing 1/8" to the inside on the unsewn side.
4. Topstitch around all four sides. (This topstitching can be decorative, if you like.) ❏

Variations

• Embroider a corner of the fashion fabric before assembling.

• Use vintage fabric or pieces of old vintage linens for coasters.

Panel Curtains

by Jennifer Jacob

This is the most basic and easy format for making a curtain. Because it never fails, it is, therefore, a perfect first sewing project.

Fabrics Recommended

cotton
voile
velveteen
brocades
silk

Level of Ability

beginner

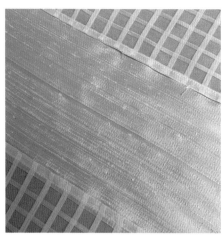

1. French seams are used on either side of the inset.

2. Hemming the sides.

fabric and notions needed:

■ Fashion fabric (I used 1-1/2 yds.)
■ Contrast fabric (for the inset – try something sheer like organza, voile, or dotted swiss)
■ Thread

cut your fabric

1. Measure the window. For the height, determine how long you want the curtain to be and how tall you wish the inset to be. For the width, allow one-and-a-half to three times the width of the window, depending on how full you wish the curtain. Add 6" to the width for side seams and 11" to the height for hems, seams, and casing.
2. Cut the fashion fabric panel(s) to size, allowing for the height of the inset in the fashion fabric piece. Cut the panel(s) where you wish to place the inset.
3. Cut the inset, adding 1" to the height for the seams.

stitch it up

1. Insert the contrast fabric inset by stitching it to the fashion fabric with French seams so the seam is finished on both sides. [**photo 1**] (See the appendix for instructions on how to make a French seam.)
2. To hem the sides, turn under 1-1/2" to the wrong side. Press. Turn under 1-1/2" to the wrong side again. Press. Edgestitch along inside edge. [**photo 2**]
3. To hem the bottom, turn fabric under 3" to the wrong side. Press. Turn fabric under another 3" to wrong side. Press. Edgestitch along inside of hem.
4. To make the top casing, turn fabric down 2" to the wrong side. Press. Turn fabric down another 2" to wrong side. Press. Edgestitch along the inside. ❏

Variations

• Sew tabs on the top.
• Bind the edges.
• Insert a strip of brilliant color.
• Adorn with keepsake pockets.

Ironing Board Cover

by Cindy Lou Who

I have never been happy with the ironing board covers available in stores. They are usually made in unappealing colors or shoddy fabrics; sometimes they don't last very long or fit very well so they slide around on the board. Since I leave my ironing board set up in my sewing studio, the appearance of the cover is important to me. If you are setting up a sewing corner, your ironing board can actually be an accent piece of furniture.

Fabrics Recommended

cotton canvas
muslin
heavy, smooth linen

Level of Ability

beginner

The best irons are heavy and produce a healthy burst of steam. Cotton pressing cloths are handy for pressing delicate and synthetic fabrics. Keep your iron clean with a commercial iron cleaner. For best results, always follow the manufacturer's instructions for cleaning.

Ironing Board Cover

This ironing board cover has a self-casing for a drawstring made by turning under the edge of the cover fabric. For a two-tone look, you could piece the cover fabric.

You will need a heat resistant surface under the fashion fabric and some sort of padding (polyester or cotton batting or foam). An option I like is to use an inexpensive (but tight-fitting) commercial ironing board cover under my custom-built beauty.

fabric and notions needed:

- 2 yds. brown paper (for pattern)
- Pencil
- 2 yds. fashion fabric - smooth cotton or Teflon-coated
- Thread
- Ruler
- Padding and heat-resistant fabric
- 5 yds. cord (for the drawstring)

Option: Use strong elastic or a long bungee cord instead of the drawstring cotton cord for a tighter fit.

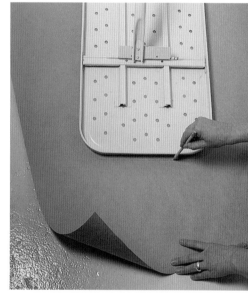

1. Making the kraft paper pattern.

make a pattern

1. Lay kraft paper on floor or large table.
2. Place the ironing board upside down on the kraft paper and trace around it with a pencil. [**photo 1**]
3. Add 4-1/2" to the edges on all sides. This is the cutting line. Cut out the paper pattern.

cut your fabric

Use the paper pattern to cut one piece of fashion fabric.

stitch it up

1. Serge or zigzag the raw edge of the fashion fabric all around the edge. Press to the wrong side 1/4".
2. Fold from the finished edge towards the wrong side of the fabric 1" and press.

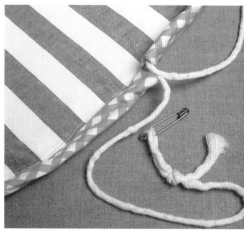

2. The cord is threaded through the casing.

3. Stitch very close to the finished edge all around, leaving a 2" opening at the center of the short straight back edge. This is the casing.
4. Thread the cord through the casing until it comes back through the other end.
5. Wrap the cover around the ironing board and pull the cord tight. Tie the ends to the legs or the frame of the ironing board. ❏

Ironing Board Cover with Contrast Bias Casing

additional supplies:

▪ 1/3 yd. contrasting fabric for bias casing

For more extensive instructions on binding an edge, see the appendix.

make a pattern

1. Lay kraft paper on floor or large table.
2. Place the ironing board upside down on the kraft paper and trace around it with a pencil. [**photo 1**]
3. Add 3" around the tracing. This is the cutting line. Cut out the paper pattern.

cut your fabric

1. Use the paper pattern to cut one piece of fashion fabric.
2. Cut contrasting bias strips 6" wide and as long as the circumference of the pattern plus a few inches extra. (Refer to the French bias instructions in the appendix.)

stitch it up

1. Fold the bias binding in half lengthwise, with wrong sides together. Starting at the center back on the straight end, tuck one short end under and, using a 1/2" seam allowance, with wrong sides together, stitch the bias binding around the edge of the cover.
2. Turn the folded bias binding over the raw edge of the cover. Turn under the raw edge of the binding and press. Edgestitch or stitch in the ditch to finish the edge, ending at the center back so the binding just meets. This is the casing. [**photo 2**]
3. Thread the cord through the casing until it comes back through the other end.
4. Wrap the cover around the ironing board and pull the cord tight. Tie the ends to the legs or the frame of the ironing board. ❏

Basket Liners

by Jennifer Jacob

I find lined baskets are convenient for storing things in my work room and studio. Basket liners are so popular that you can actually buy them inexpensively, but they probably won't match your ironing board cover or fit the baskets you already own. So here's how to make your own custom-fit basket liners. The ties for these covers are 4" wide; narrower ties can be used for smaller baskets.

Fabrics Recommended

cotton
muslin
canvas
silk

Level of Ability

beginner

"My most valuable tool is my seam ripper."

Jennifer Jacob

Basket Liners

fabrics and notions needed:

- Fashion fabric (the amount depends on the size of the basket)
- Contrast fabric for binding and ties
- Thread

make a pattern

1. Decide which sides of the basket will have ties. If the basket has a handle (or handles), the tie-side needs to be where the handle(s) are attached.
2. Measure the inside height of the basket. Measure the bottom inside dimensions of the basket. Measure the inside side dimensions of the basket. Most baskets are narrower at the bottom than at the top so measure both top **and** bottom to be sure.
3. Using these measurements, draw the patterns on paper:
   One for the bottom
   One for the 2 sides with ties
   One for the sides with flaps – double the height measurement to form the flaps
4. Add 1/2" seam allowances all the way around all the pieces.

cut your fabrics

1. From the fashion fabric, cut two flap side pieces and two tie-side pieces. Cut one bottom piece.
2. From the contrast fabric, cut four ties, each 4" wide and as long as half the width of the top of the tie side of the basket plus 15". For example, if your basket measures 12" across the side your tie length would be 6" + 15".
3. Cut enough 2" wide bias strips to go around the flaps and the top edges of the tie sides from the contrast fabric.

stitch it up

1. Bind the top edges of the tie-side panels with bias strips for a 1/2" finished binding width. (See the appendix for instructions on bias binding.)
2. With right sides together, using a 1/2" seam allowance, stitch the tie-side panels to the flap sides, stitching at sides and starting at the bottom (narrowest point). [**photo 1**]
3. With right sides together, using 1/2" seam allowance, stitch the bottom piece to the bottom edges of the sides. [**photo 2**]
4. Trim the seam allowance from the sides of the flaps, but leave the seam allowance on the ends.
5. Bind the raw edges of the flaps with the contrast bias binding, finishing at 1/2". [**photo 3**] Remember to miter the corners.
6. With right sides together, fold the ties, lining up the long edges, and stitch, using a 1/4" seam allowance.
7. Turn ties right side out and press flat, with the seam on an edge. Tuck the ends to the inside and topstitch to finish. [**photo 4**]
8. Measure halfway up the flaps and pin the ties on the wrong side at this point. Topstitch to secure. [**photo 5**] ❏

1. Stitching the tie side to the flap side.

2. Pinning the bottom to the sides.

3. Binding the edges of the flaps with contrast bias binding.

4. Tucking the ends and topstitching to finish.

5. Pinning ties to wrong side and topstitching to secure.

Reticule Jewelry Bag

by Cindy Lou Who

At the end of the 18th century, the form-fitting clothing of the day allowed no room for pockets so ladies resorted to an over-the-arm accessory to hold personal items. This small drawstring bag was known as a *reticule* or *indispensable*. They were dainty and usually made of delicate fabrics such as silk velvet or fine wool.

This design is a curtsy to that romantic era. It makes a lovely jewelry travel bag, thanks to the individual pie-shaped pockets on the inner lining.

Fabrics Recommended

silk
taffeta
satin
moire
cotton

Level of Ability

beginner

Cindy first expressed herself by
making doll clothes at age four.

Reticule Jewelry Bag

fabrics and notions needed:

- 1/4 yd. fabric of your choice (the three pattern pieces can be cut from the same fabric or any of the pattern pieces can be cut from a contrasting fabric.
- Compass
- 60" cord
- Liquid fabric sealer
- Thread

make a pattern

Use a compass to draw two circle patterns – one with a 14" diameter and one with a 9" diameter.

cut your fabrics

1. Cut one 14" circle from the fabric of your choice for the outside of the bag.
2. Cut one 14" circle from the fabric of your choice for the lining. (Use the same fabric for both or use contrasting fabrics.)
3. Cut one 9" circle for the pocket piece from either fabric. (The photo of the inside of the finished bag shows the pockets cut from the same fabric as the lining fabric. The step by step photos show the pocket piece cut from a fabric that contrasts with the lining fabric.)

stitch it up

1. Make a rolled hem at the edge of the 9" circle of lining fabric. [**photo 1**]
2. Line up the center of the 9" circle with the center of the 14" lining circle. With wrong side of the smaller circle against the right side of the larger circle, pin the smaller circle to the larger circle.
3. Sew three lines of stitching from the edge of the 9" circle through the center across to the other edge to create six pie-shaped wedges. [**photo 2**] Each wedge should be a little more than 4-1/2" wide (4.7", to be exact). This step attaches the pocket piece to the lining piece.

1. The rolled hem at the edge of the 9" circle.

2. Stitching to create six pie-shaped wedges that serve as pockets to hold jewelry.

4. Place the other fashion fabric 14" circle on top of the lining circle with right sides together. Pin. [photo 3]

5. Stitch the circles together around the edge, using a scant 1/4" seam allowance and leaving a 2" opening for turning.

6. Press flat, turn right side out, and press again. Turn the edges of the opening to the inside and press.

7. Topstitch all around the circle, being sure to catch the opening.

8. To make a casing for cords: topstitch around the circle, 1-1/4" away from the finished edge. Topstitch again 5/8" inside of the previous stitching line. [photo 4]

9. To be able to add the cording to cinch up the bag, you will need to cut two small slits opposite each other in the casing channel on the outside fabric only. Apply a liquid fabric sealer around the edges of these slits.

10. Measure and cut two 30" cords. Insert the first through the first slit, pulling it through the casing around the full circle. Tie the ends of the cording together. Repeat with the second cord through the second slit. Tie the ends together. Pull opposing ends of the cording to cinch up the bag. ❏

3. Pinning the circles together. Here the outside piece and the lining piece are cut from the same fabric.

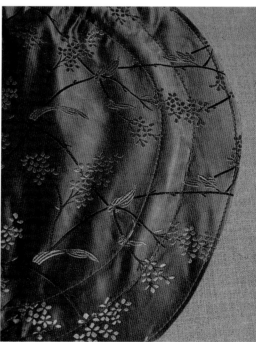

4. The lines of topstitching. The two inner lines form the casing for the drawstring.

"Goodie" Storage Bag

by Diana L. Thomas and Kristine M. Curtis

Theatre costumers call these "goodie bags." They hang along-side an actor's costume and contain all accessories that go with the costume – socks and hose in one pocket, hankies and scarves in another. Sometimes jewelry is pinned to them.

When you get used to using them, they become necessary. They are especially useful for holding sewing notions. Pack one when you travel to hold your accessories. When you arrive at your hotel, you can hang it in the closet with your clothes.

These bags can be made any length, with as many pockets as you desire. Pockets can even be different sizes as shown in the photo examples of this page and the next page.

Fabrics Recommended

canvas

corduroy

upholstery fabric

cotton twill or other sturdy
   fabric

brocade

Level of Ability

intermediate

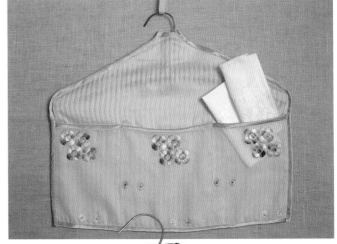

"Goodie" Storage Bag

fabrics and notions needed:

- Brown paper for pattern
- Clothes hanger
- 1 yd. fabric
- Thread
- *Options for trimming:* 1-1/3 yd. double fold bias tape, ribbon, piping, braid

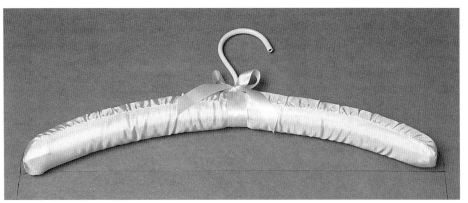

1. Using the hanger to draw the pattern.

make a pattern for goodie bag

1. Place hanger on kraft paper and draw an outline around it.
2. Add 3/4" all around it (except at the bottom) to make the cutting line.
3. Extend the pattern below the hanger on both sides to the length your goodie bag will be. *See Fig. 1.* [**photo 1**]
4. Draw a line parallel to the bottom of the hanger outline across the neck of the hanger 2" long. This is the opening for the hook of the hanger. See Figure 1.

make pocket patterns

1. Mark pocket placement on the pattern – the sizes and types of pockets are your choice. On the example in the step-by-step photos, the tops of the lower pockets are 10" from the bottom, the bottoms of the middle pockets are 5" down from the top of the square, and the top pocket is a rectangle 2-1/2" tall x 6" wide. [**photo 2**]
2. Using the marked pocket lines as guides, draw patterns for each pocket strip on kraft paper. To do this, take the pocket measurements and add 1/2" seam allowances on sides and bottom and 3/4" on the top edge for the hem. *If you are binding the tops of the pockets or using a selvage as the top edge,* don't add the 3/4" to the top. *To make pleated pockets on the bottom,* add 6" to the width.

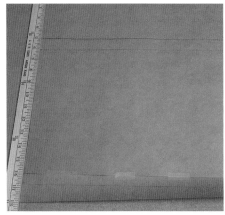

2. The pattern with the pockets drawn on it.

cut your fabric

1. Cut two bag pieces.
2. Cut 1 piece for each pocket strip if you desire pockets on only one side of your bag. Cut two pieces if you desire pockets on both front and back of bag.
3. Serge, pink, or zigzag the edges of all pieces.

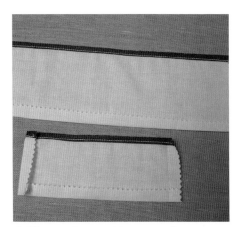

3. The pockets, with seam allowances pressed and top edges bound with bias tape.

stitch it up

1. Make a rolled hem or bind the top edge of each pocket strip. [**photo 3**]
2. If you have more than one row of pockets, on the top and middle pocket, fold the 1/2" seam allowance for the bottom edge towards the wrong side and press.
3. If the ends of a pocket piece are not going to be even with the edges of the bag, then fold and press 1/2" side seam allowances to wrong side. [**photo 3**]
4. Make a rolled hem on the top opening for the hanger on both front and back bag pieces.
5. On the bottom edge of the bag and the bottom pocket, mark the center and the quarters on the wrong side of the fabric.

Attach Bottom Pocket:

6. Pin the right side of the bottom edge of the bottom pocket to the wrong side of the bottom edge of the bag, matching center and quarter marks. [**photo 4**] If using box pleats, center the two box pleats on the quarter marks.
7. With right side of bottom pocket facing wrong side of bag front, stitch pocket to the bottom of the bag.
8. Pull the bottom pocket around to the front of bag piece and press.
9. Pin the sides of the pocket to the bag. Pin the center.
10. Sew vertical lines of stitching to divide the pockets where desired. Reinforce at top of each pocket.

Attach Any Additional Pockets:

11. Pin the middle and top pockets in place.
12. With right sides together, stitch the bottom of any pocket strips to the marked pocket lines on bag. Flip up over seam and press flat.
13. Top stitch any pocket that does not extend to the side seams (such as the top center pocket) around all three sides.
14. Sew vertical lines of stitching to divide the pockets where desired. Reinforce at top of each pocket. [**photo 5**]

Attach Front and Back of Bag:

15. Pin the front to the back, right sides together.
16. Sew up the sides, catching the pocket sides in seam and leaving the neck hole open.
17. Clip the curves. [**photo 6**] Turn right side out. Press.
18. Place the hanger hook through the hole. ❏

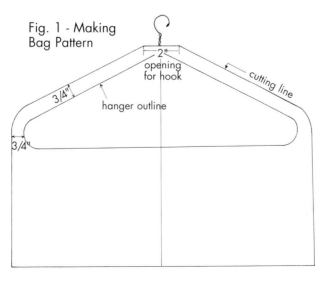

Fig. 1 - Making Bag Pattern

opening for hook

2"

cutting line

3/4"

hanger outline

3/4"

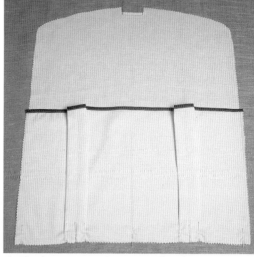

4. The bottom pocket pinned to bottom edge, right sides together, with the pleats pinned in place.

5. The pockets are sewn in place. Topstitching, using thread that matches the bias binding, divides the middle and bottom pockets.

6. Clipping the curves before turning.

Hanging Shoe Bag

by Diana L. Thomas

This project is perfect for anyone who doesn't have enough closet space for all those shoes. These hanging storage bags make super space savers in closets as well as nifty bedroom wall hangings. I have also used shoe bags for collections of gloves and for lightweight kitchen, household, or bathroom items.

The men's shoe bag in these instructions is roomier to accommodate larger shoes. The smaller woman's bag has slightly daintier measurements. You may want to make a scrap cloth pattern of one pocket to see which size works best for your shoes.

Fabrics Recommended

heavy cotton canvas
woven wool
heavier satin
medium to heavy cotton

Level of Ability

intermediate

"Everyone should at least know the basics. Sewing is a survival skill – really!"

Diana Thomas

Hanging Shoe Bag

In these instructions, the first measurements are for the woman's bag; measurements for the man's shoe bag are in parentheses that follow.

fabric and notions needed:

for a woman's shoe bag

- 1 yd. backing fabric
- 1 yd. pocket fabric
- 1/2 yd. fabric (for contrast trim) *or* 5-1/2 yds. purchased bias trim

for man's shoe bag

- 1 yd. backing fabric
- 1-1/2 yd. pocket fabric
- 1/2 yd. fabric (for contrast trim) *or* 9-1/2 yds. purchased bias trim
- Chalk or disappearing marker

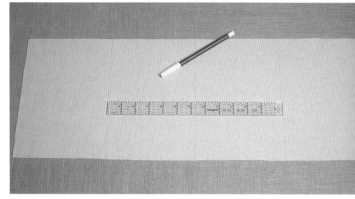

1. Marking the stitching lines on the pockets.

cut your fabric

1. From the backing fabric, cut a rectangle 18" wide x 34" tall (23-3/4" wide x 44-1/2" tall).
2. From the pocket fabric, cut three rectangles, each 25-1/2" wide x 9" tall (47" wide x 11" tall).
3. From the contrast trim fabric, cut 5-1/2 yds. of 1-1/2" wide bias strips (9-1/2 yds. of 1-1/2" wide bias strips).

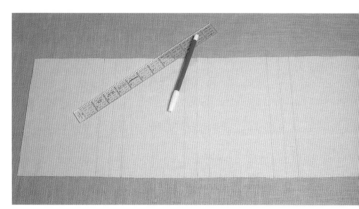

2. Marking the pleat lines on the pockets.

stitch it up

1. On the wrong side of each pocket rectangle, mark topstitching lines to divide each piece into four pockets. Using chalk or disappearing ink, mark the center line by folding the width in half. Then mark a parallel line 6-1/4" (11-3/4") from the center line on both sides of the center line. [**photo 1**]
2. On the right side of the pocket fabric, draw a line 7/8" (3") on either side of the topstitching line. [**photo 2**] On

3. Pinning and staystitching the pleats.

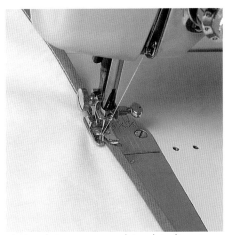

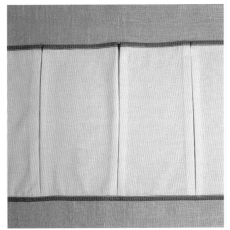

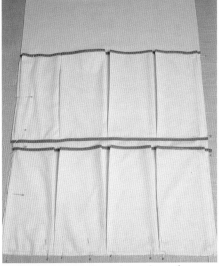

4. Applying contrast bias binding to the top of a pocket.

5. Pleats are pressed in place.

6. Pockets are pinned in place for sewing.

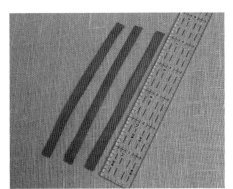

7. Three loops for hanging the bag are made from bias strips.

each outer edge, mark lines 1/4" from the edge and 1-1/8" (3-1/4") from the edge. These lines mark the pleat placements.

3. Fold the fabric at each line to the topstitch line and pin. Fold the 1-1/8" (3-1/4") mark to meet the 1/4" mark. Pin. Staystitch 1/4" up across the bottom to hold the pleats in place. [**photo 3**]

4. Bind the top of each pocket with contrast bias binding. [**photo 4**]

5. Press pleats, top to bottom. [**photo 5**]

6. Bind the bottoms of two pockets with self-bias strips.

7. Mark the center line of the backing piece.

8. Place the pockets on the backing, starting with the pocket that has the unbound bottom edge. Line up sides and bottom with the bottom edge of the backing and pin in place. Pin the topstitching lines to the backing, keeping each parallel to sides of backing (4-1/2" from edge) and matching the center lines.

9. Place the bottom of the next pocket 1" (3") above the top of this pocket, and pin. Repeat with the last pocket.

10. Topstitch each pocket in place along the sides, 1/4" from the edge, and across the bottom of each pocket. Topstitch the pocket divisions. [**photo 6**]

11. Using the contrast bias binding, bind the edges of the backing piece, catching the pocket raw edges.

12. Make hanging loops using a 15" bias strip. Fold edges toward the middle, then fold in half. Topstitch close to the edge. Cut into three 5" pieces. [**photo 7**]

13. Place hanging loops at the top edge of the wrong side of the backing. Fold each bias piece in half and place the ends to line up with the top edge of the backing and the loops to lie against the backing. Place one in the center and one 1/2" from each side. Stitch in place, using a 1/4" seam allowance.

14. Press the hanging loops up so they stand above the edge of the bag and topstitch. [**photo 8**] ❑

8. Hanging loops are attached.

Flower Pot Purse

by Cindy Lou Who

This bag reminded Cindy of a flower pot, so she dubbed it the flower pot bag. It is a clever small purse that is a perfect accessory for a dressy ensemble. These perky purses feel very youthful and a bit flirtatious. Their flat bottoms allow them to sit upright, and they are roomy enough for all your essentials.

Fabrics Recommended
satin
silk brocade

Level of Ability
advanced

Flower Pot Purse

The bag is trimmed with bias-covered piping and the handles are bias-covered cord. You can use a contrasting or matching fabric to make the cord and piping. For instructions for making piping and covering cord, see the appendix.

fabrics and notions needed:

- 25" bias-covered cord, 1/2" diameter
- 1 yd. bias piping, 1/4" diameter
- 1/4 yd. fashion fabric
- 1/4 yd. lining
- Medium weight sew-in interfacing
- Heavy weight fusible interfacing
- Brown paper for pattern
- Thread

make a pattern

1. Copy the patterns provided and enlarge the pieces as noted or enlarge to make the size bag you desire.
2. Cut patterns from kraft pattern paper.

cut your fabrics

All pattern pieces include seam allowance.

1. From fashion fabric, cut two sides and one bottom.
2. From lining fabric, cut two sides, one bottom, and two pockets.
3. Fuse four layers of the heavy weight interfacing, placing the glue side up on the bottom layer and down on all other layers. [**photo 1**]
4. From the fused interfacing layers, cut one interfacing bottom.
5. From medium weight interfacing, cut two sides.

stitch it up

1. To make the inside lining pocket, stitch the two pocket pieces, right sides together, using a 1/4" seam allowance, leaving about 1" open on one long side for turning. [**photo 2**] Press and clip the corners. Turn to the right side and press again, turning the raw edges inside.
2. Pin the pocket to the right side of one lining piece, centering the pocket on the lining about a third of the way down and placing the turning opening on the bottom. [**photo 3**] Topstitch. Make sure that the turning opening is caught in the topstitching.
3. Stitch the medium interfacing to the wrong sides of the fashion fabric side pieces, using a 1/2" seam allowance.
4. With right sides together, stitch the side seams in the fashion fabric side pieces. This creates a tube-like shape.
5. With right sides together, stitch both sides of lining side seams, using a 1/2" seam allowance.
6. Place the two bottom pieces, wrong sides together. Sandwich the interfacing bottom between these two pieces, centering it. Pin to hold. Stitch around bottom close to the interfacing through all layers, using a zipper or cording foot. Leave an even seam allowance all around. [**photo 4**]
7. Trim the seam allowance on all bottom layers to 1/2".
8. Pin the stitching line of the piping at the stitching line on the fashion fabric bottom. Clip the seam allowance of the piping to ease around the curves. Stitch. [**photo 5**]
9. Stitch piping to the top edge of the fashion fabric sides, using a 1/2" seam allowance.
10. Cut 25" of covered cord in half. (These are the handles.) Pin the handle ends in the seam allowance at the top of the fashion fabric sides between the notches. Both ends of one handle should be on the same side. [**photo 6**]

1. Fusing the stacked interfacing layers for the bottom piece.

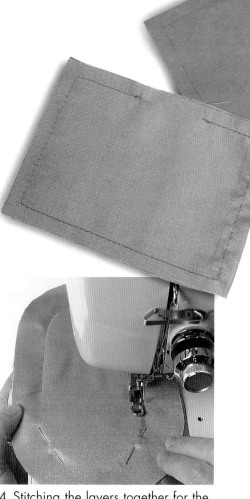

2. The pocket is stitched with an opening left for turning.

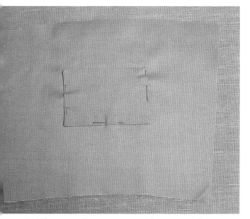

3. The pocket is pinned to one lining piece.

4. Stitching the layers together for the bottom of the bag.

Four out of five stitchers say zippers are their least favorite sewing task.

5. The bag bottom with the piping in place.

6. Covered cord handles are pinned in place.

11. Pin and stitch the right side of the lining to the right side of the fashion fabric sides, using 1/2" seam allowance. (The handles are sandwiched between them.) All seam allowances should face the same way.

12. Stitch the bottom of the fashion fabric sides to the bag bottom, right sides together.

13. Turn the bag inside out. By hand, stitch the lining of the body to the lining of the bottom. ❑

Flower Pot Bag
Patterns
(Actual Size)

Cut 2 from fashion fabric
Cut 2 from lining
Cut 2 from medium weight interfacing

Sides

Place on fold

Pocket
Cut 2 from lining

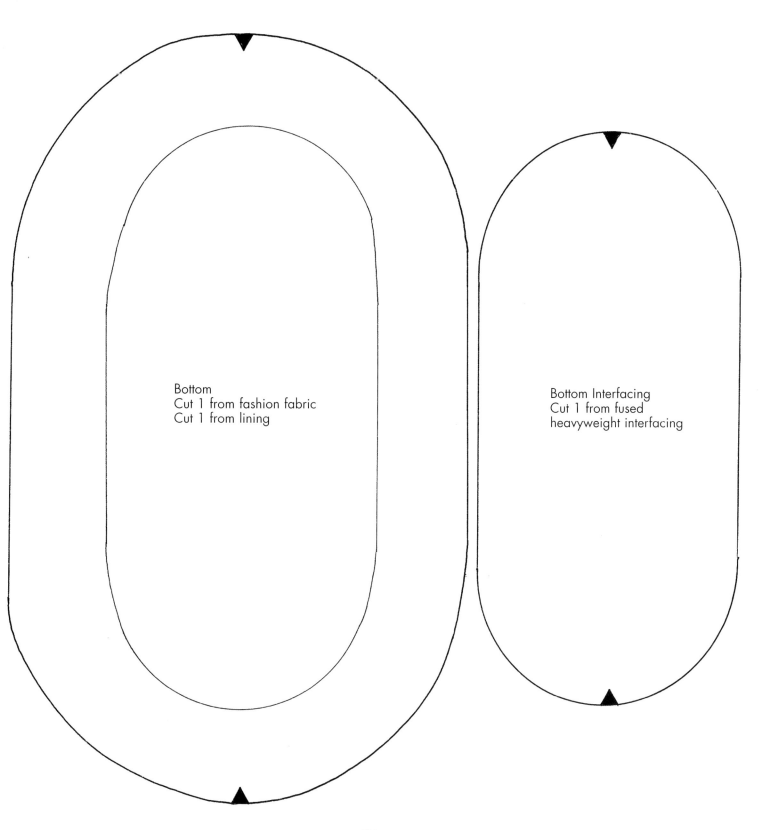

Bottom
Cut 1 from fashion fabric
Cut 1 from lining

Bottom Interfacing
Cut 1 from fused
heavyweight interfacing

Cinch Knapsack

by Renee Holland and Jennifer Jacob

A stylish purse can truly complete an outfit. This one will turn heads and elicit comments.

Fabrics Recommended

silk brocade
cotton canvas

Level of Ability

advanced

Cinch Knapsack

This bag is the happy marriage of three fabrics.

fabrics and notions needed:

▪ Kraft paper
▪ 1-1/3 yds. fabric #1 (for the front and back)
▪ 1/4 yd. fabric #2 (for the sides)
▪ 3/8 yd. fabric #3 (for the bottom, pocket, casing, and straps)
▪ 1/4 yd. fusible interfacing
▪ 1/3 yd. lining
▪ 60" cord, covered with bias strips cut from fabric #3
▪ Thread

make the pattern

See Fig. 1.
1. For the bottom, cut a rectangle 4-1/2" x 9" from kraft paper.
2. For the front and back, cut a 10" x 10" square from kraft paper.
3. For the sides, cut a rectangle 5-1/2" x 10" from kraft paper.
All pieces include a 1/2" seam allowance.

cut your fabrics

1. Using the bottom pattern, cut six layers of fusible interfacing without the 1/2" seam allowance (9" x 4-1/2").
2. Using the front and back pattern, cut two from fabric #1.
3. Using the side pattern, cut two from fabric #2.
4. Using the bottom pattern, cut one from fabric #3.
5. For the casing, cut a strip of fabric #3 that measures 28" x 4".
6. From the lining fabric, cut one bottom piece.
7. From lining fabric, cut one piece 28" x 10" for the body lining.
8. Decide what size pocket you want for the outside of your bag. Cut two pieces this size plus 1/4" seam allowance all the way around from the #3 fabric.

stitch it up

1. Fuse bottom layers of interfacing together with bottom layer glue side up and the rest glue side down. [**photo 1**]
2. Sandwich the fused interfacing between the wrong sides of bottom lining and bottom fabric pieces. Stitch closely around the interfacing, using a zipper or cording foot to snuggle up close to the interfacing. [**photo 2**]

1. Fusing the stacked interfacing layers for the bottom piece.

2. Stitching the layers together for the bottom of the bag.

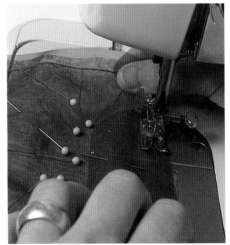
3. Making the pocket.

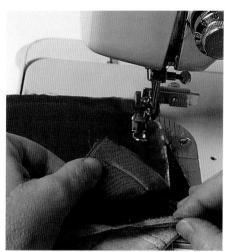

4. Stitching the front, back, and sides to the bottom.

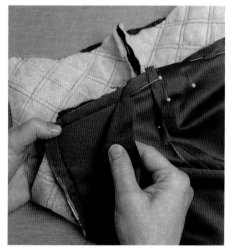

5. Pinning the bag lining to the bottom.

6. Pinning the casing to the top of the bag.

3. Pin right sides of pocket together. Stitch around three sides with 1/4" seam allowance, leaving what will be the top of the pocket open for turning. [**photo 3**] Turn right side out. Press in the 1/4" seam along the top. Topstitch the top edge closed 1/8" from edge.

4. Position the pocket on the right side of the front. Topstitch the sides and bottom 1/8" from the edge to secure.

5. With right sides together, stitch the sides to the front, using a 1/2" seam allowance. Then stitch the sides to the back, making a tube. Press all seams open.

6. With right sides together, stitch the bottom piece to the bottom of all four sides of the bag, using a 1/2" seam allowance. *Tip:* It may be easier if you pin and stitch one side at a time. [**photo 4**]

7. Stitch the body of the lining, using a 1/2" seam allowance to make a tube.

8. Pin the bag lining to the bottom with the right side of the lining to the lining side of the bottom. [**photo 5**] Stitch, using a 1/2" seam allowance. Turn the bag right side out.

9. Line up the top of the lining with the top of the bag, wrong sides together. Stitch together 1/2" from the top.

10. Fold and press in 1/4" each short side of the 28" x 4" strip of fabric #3. Fold over and press again. (This is the casing.) Topstitch to hem these ends.

11. Starting at the center of the back panel, with right sides together, pin the casing around the top of the bag. [**photo 6**] Stitch, using a 1/2" seam allowance. Press the seam up. Fold under the other side of the casing 1/2" and press.

12. Fold the pressed edge 1/4" below the line where the casing is stitched to the bag. Pin and stitch in the ditch from the right side.

13. Tack the opening of the casing closed 1/2" above the attachment line.

14. Thread the 60" of covered cord through the casing. Line up the ends of the cord and pull to even up inside the casing.

15. Stitch the end of the cord coming out of the right side to the right bottom back corner through all layers of the bag with the raw edge facing up. Fold long cord over raw edge and stitch 1/2" up to finish the end. Repeat for the end of the cord coming from the left. ❏

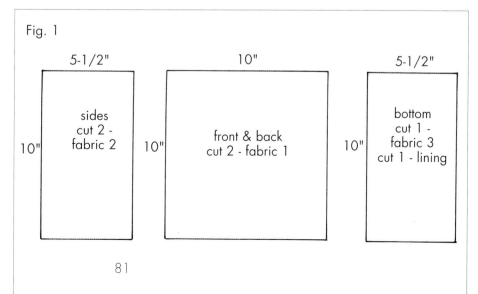

Fig. 1

5-1/2"	10"	5-1/2"
10" sides cut 2 - fabric 2	10" front & back cut 2 - fabric 1	10" bottom cut 1 - fabric 3 cut 1 - lining

Drawstring Tote Bag

by Jennifer Jacob

This sack-style bag can be customized to any size – small enough for a lunch bag or large enough for a carry-on tote. Numerous strap and trim variations make this a very versatile design. A simple seam establishes the depth of the bag and allows it to sit flat on the bottom. It would make a great club fundraising project with your special name or logo on the side.

Fabrics Recommended

canvas
denim
tapestry
mesh
microfiber such as tencel

Level of Ability

beginner

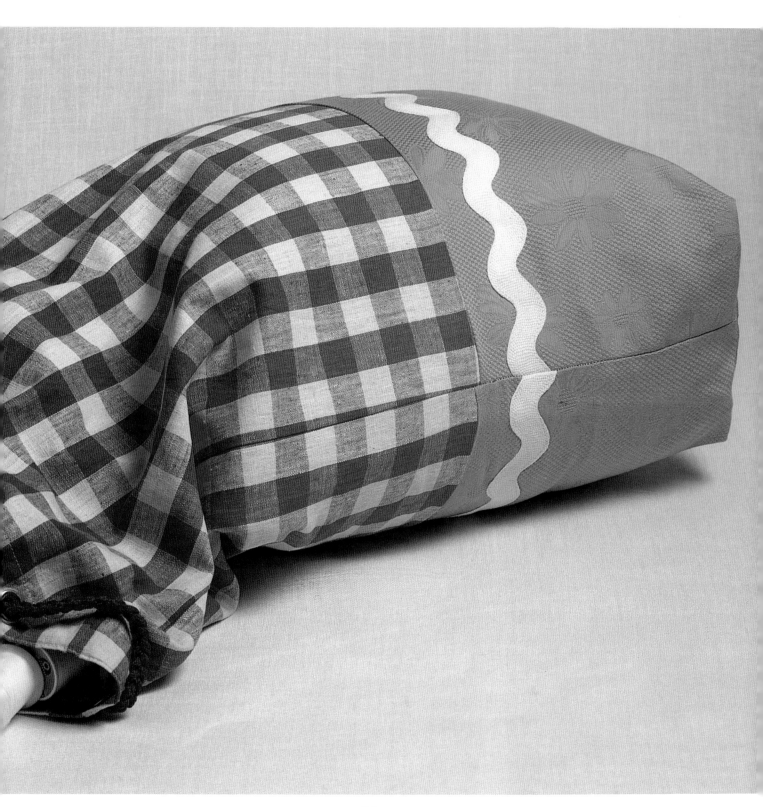

Drawstring Tote Bag

fabrics and notions needed:

- 1/2 yd. fashion fabric (for sides)
- 1/2 yd. contrast fabric (for the bottom section)
- Thread
- 2 yds. cording
- 8 brass grommets, 3/4"
- Grommet setter
- 1 yd. large rickrack trim *(optional)*

1. The contrast fabric (which forms the bottom) is stitched to the fashion fabric.

cut your fabrics

1. From the contrast fabric, cut one rectangle 18" x 24" for bottom.
2. From the fashion fabric, cut two rectangles, each 18" x 20" for sides.

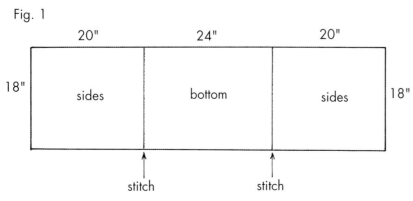

2. The side seams are pinned, ready for stitching.

stitch it up

1. With right sides together, using a 1/2" seam allowance, stitch the 18" side of one fashion fabric rectangle to EACH 18" side of the contrast fabric rectangle. [**photo 1**] *See Fig. 1.*
2. Press all seam allowances toward the contrast fabric.
3. With right sides together, fold the contrast fabric piece so the fashion fabric pieces are lying on top of each other and the seams are lined up. [**photo 2**]
4. Stitch the sides, using a 1/2" seam allowance. Press open the seams (unless you're serging them – if you are, press to one side).
5. Keep piece wrong side out. Flatten out bag so that one of the side seams is centered and facing you vertically. Along the side seam, measure down 8"

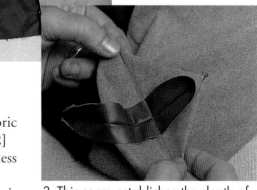

3. This seam establishes the depth of the bag and gives it a flat bottom.

Fig. 1

20"	24"	20"
sides	bottom	sides

18" ... 18"

↑ stitch   ↑ stitch

Fig. 2

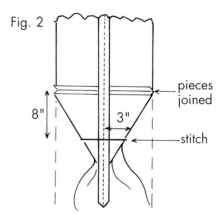

pieces joined

8"   3"

stitch

84

from the horizontal seam where the sides are joined to the bottom. Draw a line perpendicular to the side seam 3" out on both sides. Flatten the fabric to form a triangle. Stitch across the lines you've just drawn. [**photo 3**] Trim off triangle. This creates the flat bottom. Do this on other side seam side. *See Fig. 2.*

6. Along top of bag, fold down 1-1/2" and press. Fold down again 1-1/4" and press. Top stitch along both folds, stitching close to the folds.

7. Mark spacing for grommets. They are even spaced along the top band of the bag. Set grommets using a grommet setter. Run cord through grommets.

8. *Optional Rick-Rack Trim: Cut trim in two 18" wide pieces. Sew trim to bottom piece before sides are sewn together.* ❑

Braided Strap Tote

This bag is made the same way as the Drawstring Tote Bag on the previous page. Instead of adding the grommets and drawstring cord, you will add braided straps instead.

additional supplies:

▨ Woven braid, 2-1/2" wide, 3-1/2 yards.

cut and stitch

1. From the contrast fabric, cut one rectangle 12" x 15" for bottom.

2. From the fashion fabric, cut two rectangles, each 11" x 15" for sides.

3. Sew the side pieces to the bottom matching the 15" sides.

4. Along top of bag, fold down 1/4" and press. Fold down again 1" and press. Top stitch along both folds, stitching close to the folds.

5. Cut pieces of woven braid for the straps, cutting the length of your choice. Sew to both bag sides.

6. Sew additional pieces of braid on the bag sides, covering the strap bottoms and covering the seam that joins the top to the bottom.

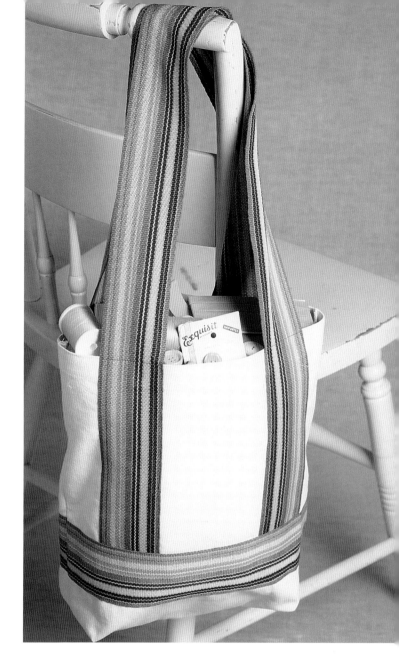

7. With right sides together, fold the contrast fabric piece so the fashion fabric pieces are lying on top of each other and the seams are lined up.

8. Stitch the sides, using a 1/2" seam allowance. Press open the seams (unless you're serging them – if you are, press to one side).

9. Keep piece wrong side out. Flatten out bag so that one of the side seams is centered and facing you. Along one of the side seams, measure down 3-1/2" from the horizontal seam where the sides are joined to the bottom. Draw a line perpendicular to the side seam 2" out on both sides. Flatten the fabric to form a right triangle. Stitch across the lines you've just drawn. [**photo 3**] Trim. This creates the flat bottom. ❑

Reversible Sling Shoulder Purse

by Jennifer Jacob

Jennifer road tested this bag on her last jaunt to far-off lands. It proved to be everything a travel bag needs to be and was declared a resounding success.

Fabrics Recommended

canvas
corduroy
denim
cotton
microfiber

Level of Ability

intermediate

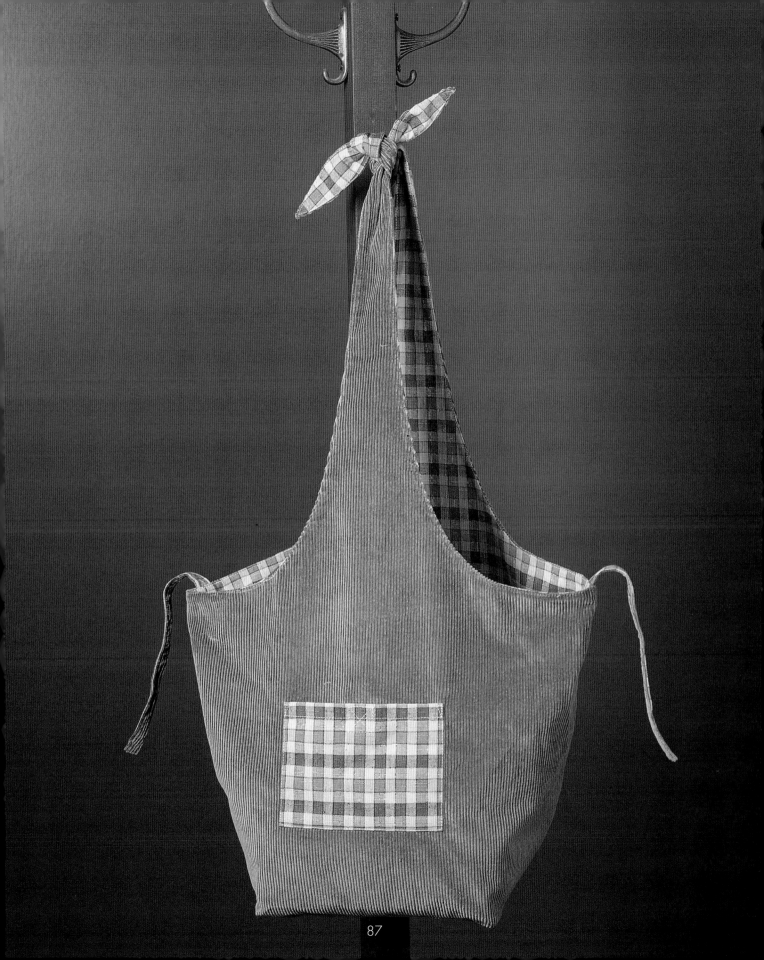

Reversible Sling Shoulder Purse

fabrics and notions needed:

- 1 yd. solid-color fabric
- 1 yd. print fabric
- 2 squares of hook-and-loop closure, 1"
- Brown paper for pattern
- Thread

make a pattern

1. Enlarge the pattern provided to the correct size.
2. Cut out a kraft paper pattern.

cut your fabrics

1. From each fabric, cut two 10" x 10" square bottom pieces. Mark the center of each side of the square. [**photo 1**]
2. From each fabric, cut two body pieces from pattern provided.
3. From each fabric, cut a 6" x 7" rectangle for the pocket.
4. From each fabric, cut two 1" x 10" strips for the ties.

You should have four bodies, two bottoms, two pockets and four ties – in all.

stitch it up

Make Ties:

1. Place one solid tie piece and one print tie piece with right sides together. Stitch the long sides to make one tie, using a 1/4" seam allowance. [**photo 2**] Trim the seam allowance to 1/8" and turn right side out. Tuck one end back inside and topstitch to finish. Repeat for other tie.

Add Pockets:

2. Hem one 7" side of each pocket by folding in 1/2" twice and topstitching. [**photo 3**]
3. Center one of the prickly sides of the hook-and-loop squares on the wrong side of the hemmed edge of each

1. Marking the center of each side of the bottom square.

pocket. Topstitch in the shape of an X across the square. [**photo 4**]

4. Fold in the other three sides of each pocket 1/2" and press. Center the pocket on one body piece of the opposite fabric, with the wrong side of the pocket to the right side of the body. Topstitch, reinforcing the top corners with a triangle. [**photo 5**] Repeat for the other pocket, again applying to the contrasting fabric.
5. Align the fuzzy side of the hook-and-loop square on the body piece with the prickly opposite piece. Topstitch in place.

Assemble:

6. With right sides together, stitch together the sides of the two body pieces of the solid fabric, using a 1/2" seam allowance.
7. Repeat with the body pieces of the print fabric.

8. Press the seams open. Staystitch 1/4" from the edges of all four body pieces.

9. Pin the matching bottom to the seamed body, lining up the center marks on the bottom with the seams and centers of the body. Stitch, using a 1/2" seam allowance. [**photo 6**]

10. Repeat with the other fabric.

11. Fold over and press the edges of the bodies on the staystitching lines.

12. Line up the pressed edges of the bag bodies, wrong sides together, and pin. Place the unfinished ends of the ties 1/2" into this seam at the side seams of the bodies. Pin. [**photo 7**] Edgestitch the two bodies together, catching the ties.

13. Line up the bottom corners of the bag. Neatly tack the two layers together by hand.

14. Knot the ends of the straps together. Tie the little ties to hold the bag shut. ❏

2. Stitching the long sides of a tie.

3. Hemming one side of a pocket.

4. Topstitching the hook-and-loop square on a pocket.

5. Topstitching a pocket in place.

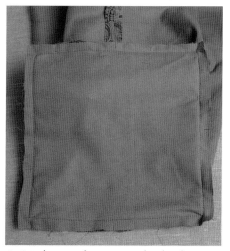
6. Stitching a bottom to the body.

7. Pinning a tie in place.

Pattern for Reversible Sling Purse Body

Enlarge at 230% for actual size

Cut 2 from each fabric.

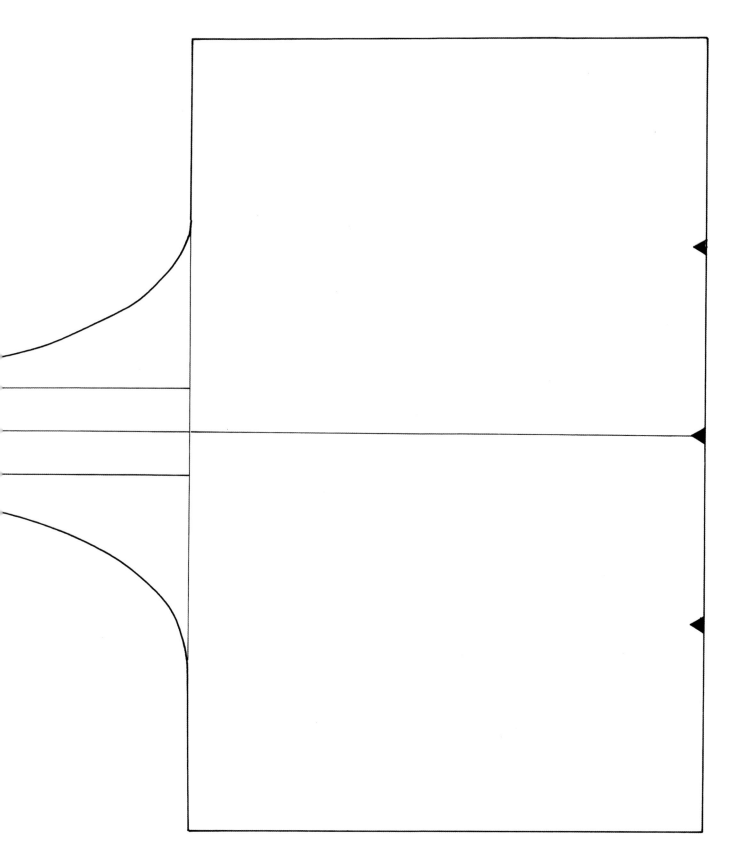

Fleece Hat, Scarf, and Mittens

by Jennifer Jacob

These are easy, fun, and practical. Jennifer first made them as Christmas gifts. She has elaborated on the theme and added her own stylish touches.

Fabrics Recommended

fleece
cotton knit
spandex

Level of Ability

beginner

Fleece Hat, Scarf, and Mittens

fabrics and notions needed:

- 1 yd. synthetic fleece, 60" wide
- Scrap of fleece in a contrasting color
- 4" elastic, 1/4"
- Button
- Thread
- Brown paper for pattern

make the scarf

Finished size is 9" x 60".

1. Cut a 9" piece of 60" width from fabric. Trim off selvages.
2. Finish edges with serger, zigzag, or hand blanket stitch. [**photo 1**]

1. The scarf, with finished edges.

make the hat

1. Cut a piece of fleece 24" wide (the top and bottom) by 22" long (the sides).
2. With right sides together, fold in half. Serge or zigzag together the 22" sides. [**photo 2**]
3. Serge or zigzag around one 24" side (this is the bottom). Measure up 4" from the bottom edge and mark. Fold on this line, wrong sides together. Topstitch to form the cuff of the hat. Fold cuff back up on the right side. [**photo 3**]
4. Measure 4" from the top edge and mark. Sew a gathering stitch on this line by hand or machine.
5. Pull the gathering stitch as tightly as possible and secure. [**photo 4**]
6. Cut a piece of contrasting fleece 1" x 8". Serge or zigzag the edges. Wrap this piece of fleece around the gathered top of the hat as tightly as you can, folding under the outer end. Stitch in place by hand. Trim with a button.
7. Above the contrast piece, cut the top of the hat every 3/4" to make fringe. [**photo 5**]

make the mittens

1. Make a pattern by placing your hand on kraft paper with your fingers together and thumb extended at a 90 degree angle. Trace around your hand, rounding over the tops of your fingers to create a smooth curve. To the tracing, add 3/4" all the way around and add 2" at the wrist to make a cuff.
2. Cut out two rights and two lefts from fleece. (Flip the pattern to make one for the opposite hand.)
3. Cut two 2" pieces of 1/4" elastic. [**photo 6**]
4. Take one right and one left. (These will be the bottoms of each hand.) On the wrong side, pin one end of the elastic to the edge of the fabric on the wrist line. Stretch the elastic as much as possible and, using a zigzag stitch, stitch it on the wrist line. Snip off any excess elastic.
5. Place one bottom and one top, wrong sides together. Serge or zigzag together around all sides except (of course!) the wrist opening. [photo 7]
6. Turn the mitten right side out. Serge, zigzag, or blanket stitch around the wrist edge. ❏

2. Seaming the hat.

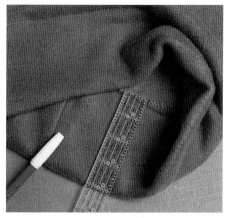

3. Measuring the hem of the hat that forms the cuff.

4. Gathering the top of the hat.

5. Cutting the fringe at the top of the hat.

6. The pieces of the mittens, shown with the pattern.

7. One mitten, seamed together, before turning.

Variations

• Use a patterned fleece. Center a motif on the top of the hand when you cut out the mittens.

• Use two contrasting colors of fleece, as shown in the photograph on pages 92-93. Make one side of the mittens, the band on the hat, and the cuff of the hat in the contrasting color. Use narrow strips cut from the contrasting color to make fringe for the ends of the scarf.

Baby Bibs and Burp Cloths

by Renee Holland

That special baby will feel so loved with these custom made and creatively conceived bibs and burp cloths. They are the perfect, unique shower gift or new baby present — washable and easy to care for. They may well become treasured keepsakes, handed down to the next generation.

Fabrics Recommended

terrycloth
chenille
flannel

Level of Ability

beginner

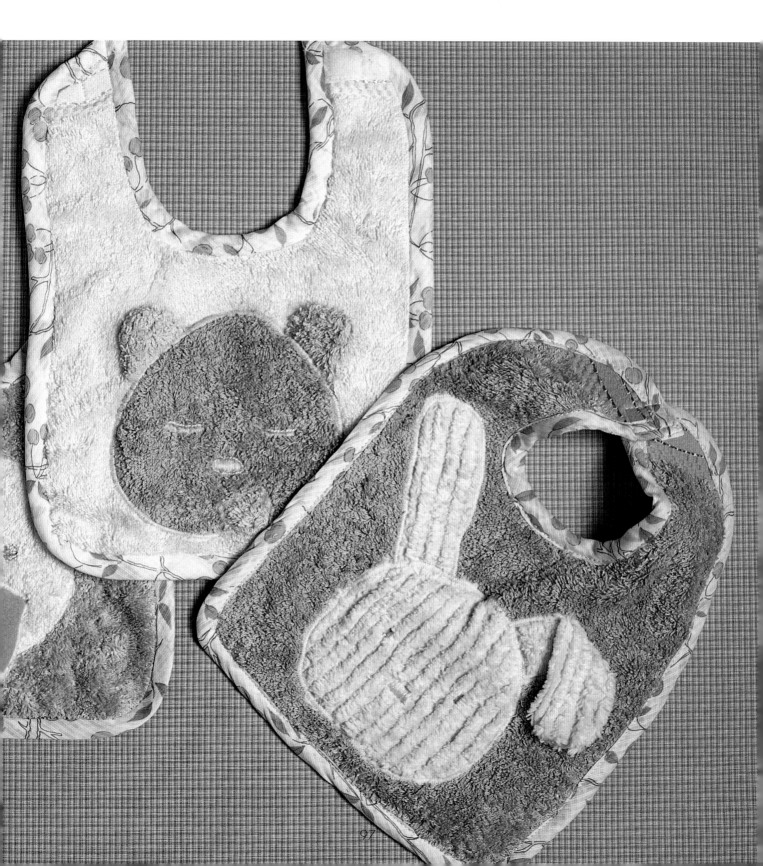

Baby Bibs and Burp Cloths

fabric and notions needed:

for bib

- 2 towels in contrasting colors
- 2 yds. of purchased bias binding *or* 1/2 yd. fabric to make bias binding
- 1" hook-and-loop tape
- *Optional:* 1/8 yd. fleece (for animal ears, beak, tongue)
- Thread

for burp cloth

- Cloth diapers or 1/3 yard flannel
- 1/4 yd. fabric (for binding) or 1-1/3 yards purchased bias binding

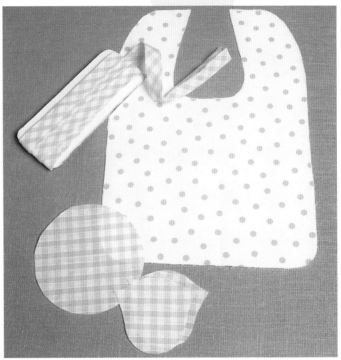

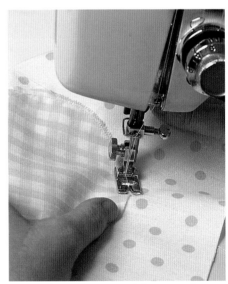

1. Pieces for a bib made from two woven fabrics.

make the bib

1. Cut the bib shape from a towel using pattern provided. Cut the pieces for an applique face (duck, bear, or bunny) from a towel in a contrasting color.
2. Cut out the features (beak, ears, tongue) from towel scraps or fleece.
3. *Option:* Make 2 yds. bias binding from 2" wide bias strips of fabric (to finish at 1/2" wide). See appendix for instructions on making bias binding.
4. Center the applique on the bib and baste in place. Complete by zigzag stitching along the edge of the applique.
5. For the animals parts (ears, tongue, or beak), for each piece – place right sides together and stitch around the edges. Turn right side out, and press.
6. Position animal parts on the bib; baste, then zigzag in place. [**Photo 2**] Some pieces you will want to stitch down and some you will want to stitch only one end to attach it. For example. the duck's bill and the bunny's ear are stitched down at the base so that the part can be dimensional.
7. Stitch eyes using a satin stitch.
8. Bind the outer edges of the bib with the bias binding.
9. Cut two 1" lengths of hook-and-loop tape (one female, one male). Position with the fuzzy side on the overlap and the prickly side on the underlap. Stitch around the edges of the strips, attaching them to the bib. Be sure the fuzzy side is towards the baby's skin.

2. Stitching the animal face applique.

make the burp cloths

1. Cut 2 12" x 12" pieces of diaper or flannel.
2. Pin right sides together and stitch along all edges, leaving 2" open for turning. Turn and press opening to inside.
3. Bind the edges of each piece with bias binding. See the appendix for binding instructions. ❑

Variation: Other Fabrics

• Use woven fabrics for the bib. Cut the bib from one fabric. Cut the animal face applique from another fabric. Make bias binding from the same fabric as the animal face. [**photo 1**] Baste the face in place, then zigzag the edge. [**photo 2**]

"It is important to perpetuate the 'hand arts' by teaching and encouraging children to love fabrics."

Cindy Lou Who

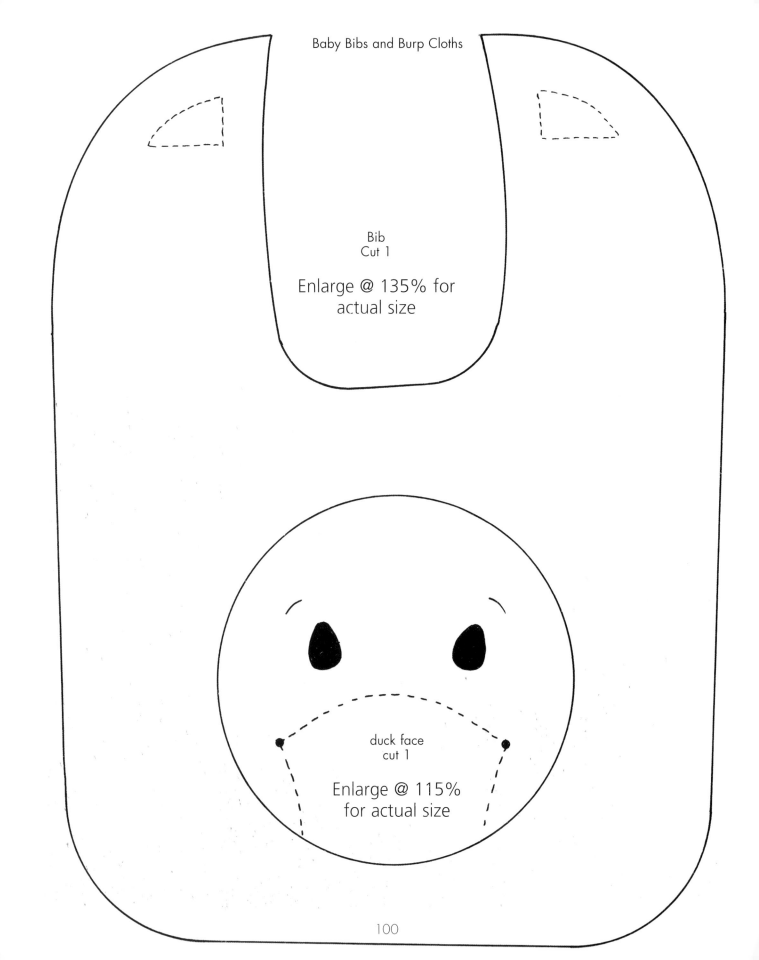

Baby Bibs and Burp Cloths

Bib
Cut 1

Enlarge @ 135% for
actual size

duck face
cut 1

Enlarge @ 115%
for actual size

Enlarge @ 115% for
actual size

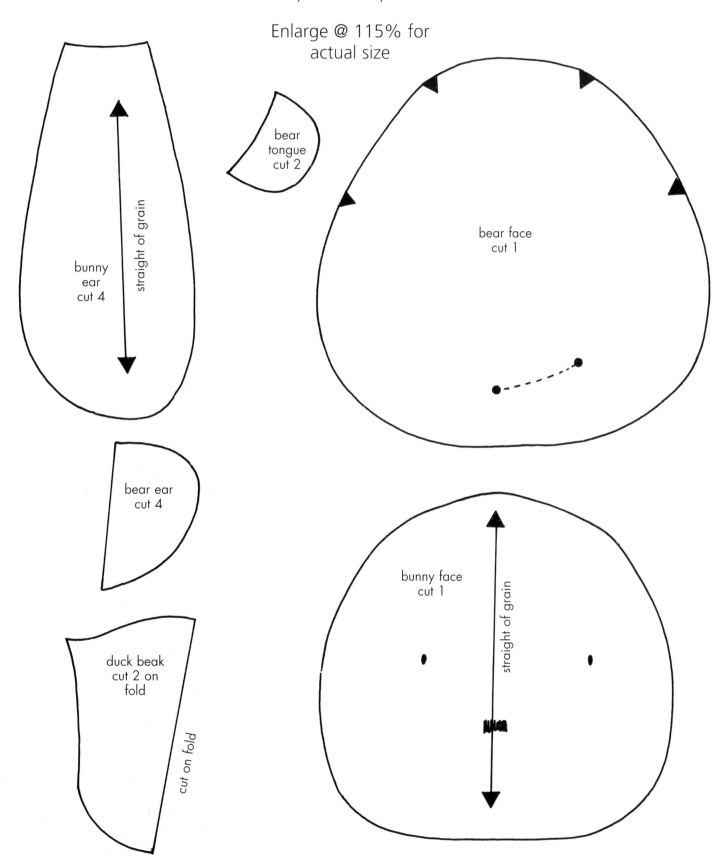

bear
tongue
cut 2

bunny
ear
cut 4

straight of grain

bear face
cut 1

bear ear
cut 4

duck beak
cut 2 on
fold

cut on fold

bunny face
cut 1

straight of grain

Sachets by Cindy Lou Who

Fill these with fragrant herbs and spices and place them in all your drawers and suitcases.

Fabrics Recommended

organza
chiffon
silk
lightweight linen

Level of Ability

beginner

fabrics and notions needed:

- Fabric scraps
- 1/4 yd. silk organza or chiffon (for the lining)
- Thread
- 1/2 yd. ribbon, 1/4" or 1/2" wide (for tie)
- Fragrant herbs or spices

cut your fabrics

1. Cut three 2-1/2" x 7" strips.
2. Cut one 6" x 7" rectangle of lining fabric.

stitch it up

1. With right sides together, using a 1/4" seam allowance, stitch together the three strips. Trim seams closely and press to one side. (This is the outside of the sachet.) [**photo 1**]
2. With right sides together, using a 1/4" seam allowance, stitch the pieced fabric to the lining along one long (7") edge. Press seam to one side.
3. Fold in half lengthwise, right sides together, to make a fabric tube. Stitch. [**photo 2**]
4. Fold the lining over the pieced outside, wrong sides together. Line up the bottom.
5. Pin and stitch all layers together. Serge or zigzag the bottom to finish the edge. [**photo 3**] Turn right side out.
6. Stitch the center of the ribbon to the side seam 1" down from the top. [**photo 4**]
7. Fill the sachet with herbs (lavender is a good choice) or spices. Tie the ribbon around the top to tightly close it. ❏

1. The pieced fabric for the sachet and the lining.

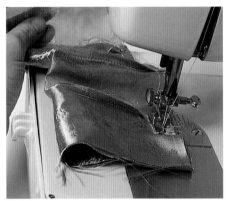

2. Stitching the long seam.

3. The sachet, lining side out, showing the stitched seam and the serged bottom.

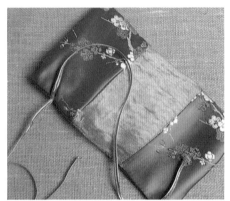

4. Attaching the ribbon to the top.

Bottle Gift Bag

by Cindy Lou Who

This project is a classy lined cover for a one-liter bottle. Simply place the bottle in the bag and tie the attached cord around the neck of the bottle. The beauty of this bag is the fold down top that reveals a lovely lining. You could expand the pattern to accommodate any size gift. I also like to fill a bag like this with small gifts – almost like a Christmas stocking – as a special, personal birthday present.

Fabrics Recommended

silk

organza

lamé

Level of Ability

beginner

fabric and notions needed:

- 15" x 14-1/2" piece of fashion fabric
- 15" x 13-1/2" piece of lining fabric
- 28" cord or ribbon

stitch it up

1. Line up the 14-1/2" sides of the fashion fabric with right sides together. Stitch, using a 1/2" seam allowance. Line up the 13-1/2" sides of the lining fabric and stitch, using a 1/2" seam allowance.

2. Turn fashion fabric right side out. Leave lining fabric inside out. Place lining inside fashion fabric, with right sides together. Pin one edge of each fabric together. Stitch, using a 1/2" seam allowance, to make a tube.

3. Pull tube so that the wrong sides of both fabrics are showing. Press seam allowance to the lining side.

4. Tuck the right side of the fashion fabric inside so the right side of the lining is on the outside. Align the open edges and pin, with the seams inside the layers. Press the top edge. (The fashion fabric will overlap the fold.)

5. Stitch the bottom edge. If you're using a four-thread serger, the edge is finished. If you're not, finish the seam.

6. Fold the bottom of the bag to create a triangle on each edge of the seam. Press flat. Stitch 1" in from the point on each side.

7. Knot the ends of the cord. Find the center. Position on the seam of the bag on the outside 1-1/2" from the top edge. Machine stitch at the seam to secure. ❏

Eyeglasses Case

by Diana L. Thomas

Here's a lovely way to store your fashion eyewear. These soft little cases take only a scrap of fabric. They're simple to make and would be a lovely gift.

Fabrics Recommended

silk dupioni
silk brocade

Level of Ability

beginner

Eyeglasses Case

fabrics and notions needed:

■ 1/8 yd. fashion fabric
■ 1/8 yd. lining
■ 1/8 yd. baby flannel (for interlining)
■ Thread

cut your fabrics

When cutting out the pattern from the fashion fabric and flannel, the slanted edge should be on the upper left corner. Flip the pattern to cut the lining. A 1/4" seam allowance is included. Transfer the pattern provided to the fashion fabric, flannel interlining, and lining fabric. Cut out on the traced lines.

stitch it up

1. Place the fashion fabric and lining with right sides together. Place the flannel interlining with its right side to the wrong side of the fashion fabric. Pin all the layers together.
2. Sew the pieces together leaving a 2" opening for turning. Clip the corner seam allowances. [**photo**]
3. Holding the flannel and fashion fabric together, turn right side out. Slipstitch the opening closed and press.
4. Fold case in half. Pin along the side and bottom. Leaving the angled end open, slipstitch the bottom and sides together. ❏

Quilted Case Variation

1. Cut out fabrics.
2. Place the flannel interlining on the wrong side of the fashion fabric. Pin the layers together.
3. On the interlining, lightly mark a quilting pattern or use the fabric design to guide the quilting. Machine quilt the layers together.
4. Pin the lining to the quilted fashion fabric, right sides together. Stitch the case, following steps 2 through 4, of the Eyeglass Case instructions given previously. ❏

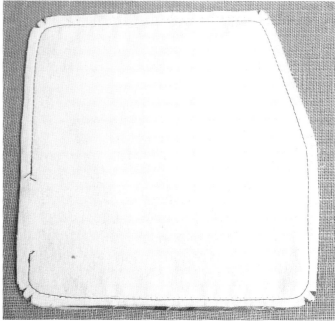

This shows the fabric layers, stitched together with the corners clipped. The flannel interlining is on top.

Beaded Case Variation

1. Cut out fabrics.
2. Place the fashion fabric and lining with right sides together. Place the flannel interlining with its right side to the wrong side of the fashion fabric. Pin all the layers together.
3. Sew the pieces together leaving a 2" opening for turning. Clip the corner seam allowances. [**photo**]
4. Holding the flannel and fashion fabric together, turn right side out. Slipstitch the opening closed and press.
5. Bead the case, either using the fabric design as a guide or sewing beads randomly on the outside of the case. Be sure to only stitch the fashion fabric as you sew on the beads.
6. Fold it in half. Pin along the side and bottom. Leaving the angled end open, slipstitch the bottom and sides together. ❏

Pattern (Actual Size)

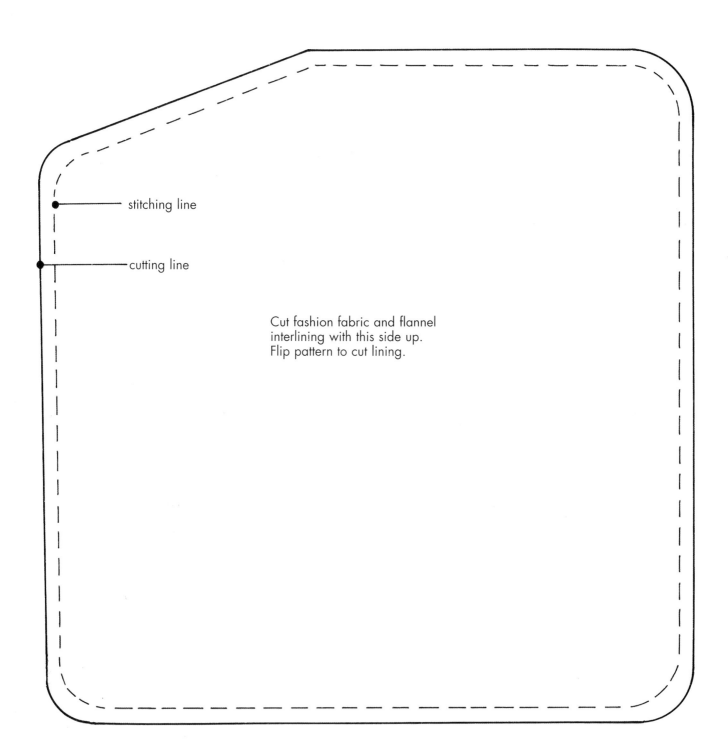

stitching line

cutting line

Cut fashion fabric and flannel
interlining with this side up.
Flip pattern to cut lining.

Sleep Mask and Neck Pillow

by Jennifer Jacob

On airplanes, I constantly see people with sleep masks and neck pillows, but I have NEVER seen any as stylish as these. Start your own trend and carry or give these elegant travel necessities.

Fabrics Recommended

silk brocade
silk dupioni
washable fleece
terrycloth
velvet

Level of Ability

beginner

Neck Pillow

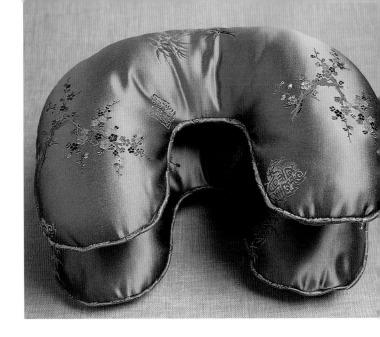

fabric and notions needed:

- ▨ 1/2 yd. fabric
- ▨ polyester stuffing
- ▨ matching or contrast piping
- ▨ Thread

cut your fabrics

Using the pattern provided, cut two pieces.

stitch it up

1. Baste piping 1/4" from edge of one piece.
2. With right sides together, stitch pieces together using 1/4" seam allowance. Leave an unstitched opening between the notches for turning and stuffing. [photo 1]

3. Clip the curves and the seam allowance as needed. [photo 1]
4. Turn right side out.
5. Stuff to desired firmness.
6. Slipstitch the opening closed. ❏

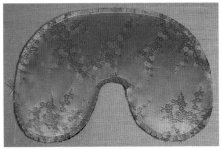

1. Neck pillow with sewn seam and an opening for stuffing.

2. Neck pillow variation with zipper inserted.

Relaxation Pillow Variation

additional supplies:

- ▨ 9" zipper
- ▨ 1/2 yd. muslin
- ▨ Lavender, buckwheat hulls, or millet or a combination (for filling)

cut your fabrics

Using the pattern provided, cut out two pieces from muslin and two pieces from the fabric.

stitch it up

1. With right sides together, stitch muslin pieces together using 1/4" seam allowance. Leave an unstitched opening between the notches for turning and stuffing.
2. Clip the curves and the seam allowance as needed. Turn right side out.
3. Stuff to desired firmness with lavender or buckwheat hulls or millet or a combination.
4. Slipstitch the opening closed.
5. Baste piping 1/4" from edge of one piece of cover fabric.
6. Set a zipper between the notches of the covering fabric, using 1/4" seam allowance and following the package instructions. Open the zipper.
7. Stitch the pillow seam, using a 1/4" seam allowance. Turn right side out through the zipper. [photo 2]
8. Insert the filled muslin pillow and zip it up! ❏

Sleep Mask

Sweet dreams! If the combination of the fashion fabric and baby flannel/soft cotton does not block light, add a third (center) layer of tightly woven dark cotton. For more extensive instructions on making and applying bias binding, see the appendix.

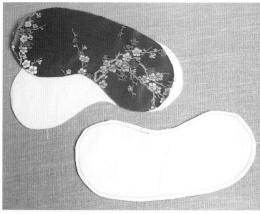

1. The pieces of the sleep mask, separately *top*, and stitched together with lining on top, *bottom*.

fabrics and notions needed:

- 1/4 yd. fabric (for top)
- 1/4 baby flannel or soft cotton (for lining)
- 24" of 1/2" (purchased or homemade) bias tape in a contrast fabric
- 2 pieces of 1/4" wide elastic, each 14" long
- *Optional:* tightly woven dark cotton (for interlining)

cut your fabrics

Cut one mask pattern from the top fabric and one from the lining fabric. *Option:* Cut a third piece from dark woven cotton.

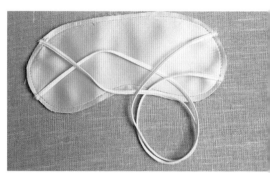

2. The elastic straps are pinned in place before the bias binding is attached.

stitch it up

1. With wrong sides together pin together the layers of fabric, and stitch around the edge, using a 1/4" seam allowance. Trim the seam allowance to 1/8". [**photo 1**]
2. Mark the strap attachment points on the back piece. Pin the elastic straps at these points so the straps are parallel across the back of the mask. Make sure the ends of the elastic face the seam allowance. Tack the straps by machine on the stitching line. [**photo 2**]
3. Bind the edges of the mask with the bias tape, covering the stitching 1/4" from the edge. *Tip:* It works best to press the bias binding around the curves as you pin. ❏

Variations

- Bead or embroider the fashion fabric side.

- Use a quilted fashion fabric or machine quilt the fabric you've chosen.

- Use a sheer fabric or lace for the top fashion layer and a second solid fashion fabric for the middle layer.

Pattern for Sleep Mask

(Actual Size)

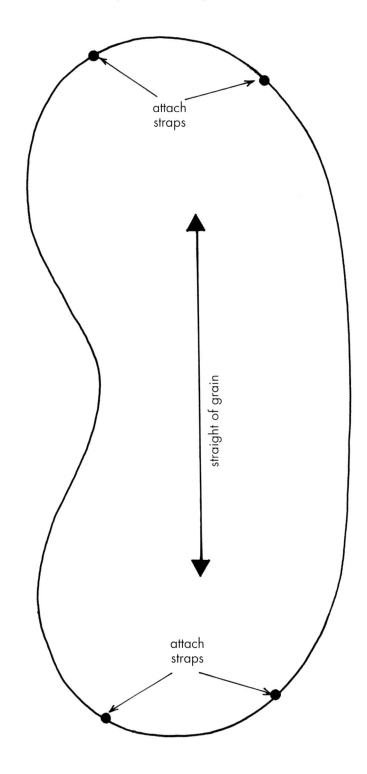

attach
straps

straight of grain

attach
straps

Pattern for Neck Pillow

Enlarge at 175% for actual size

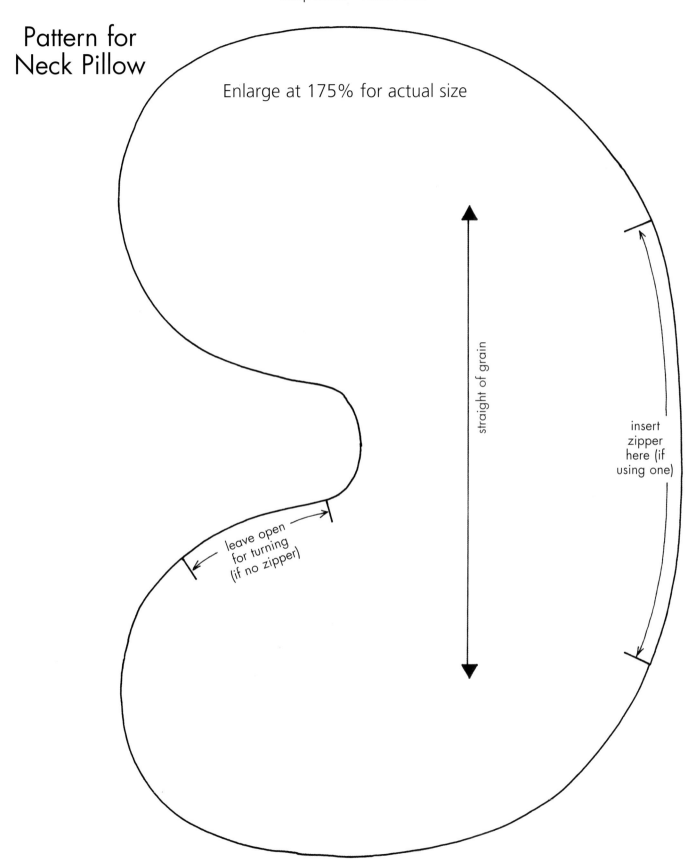

straight of grain

insert zipper here (if using one)

leave open for turning (if no zipper)

Glossary of Basic Terms

Cut Edge

The correct place to *cut* the fabric. It is the unfinished edge that cutting creates, rather than the *finished* edge.

Finished Edge

This is the edge of the fabric after it is seamed, hemmed, or otherwise *finished*.

Seam Allowance

The measurement from the edge of the fabric to the line of stitching is the seam allowance. Most projects in this book have a 1/2" seam allowance.

Fashion Fabric

The main fabric used to make a project.

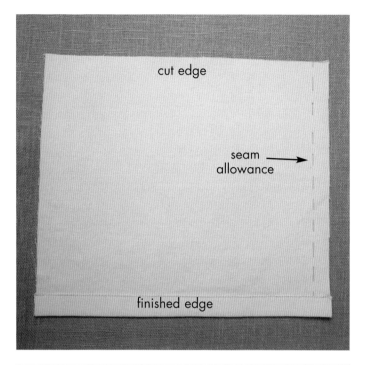

Basic Stitches

Baste

To stitch **temporarily** with long stitches, either by hand or machine.

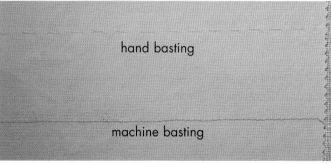

Blanket stitch/buttonhole stitch

Work this stitch from left to right with the edge of the fabric towards you. Secure the first stitch at the edge of the fabric. For the next stitch, with the needle pointing toward you, go through the right side of the fabric, keeping the thread below and behind the needle. Continuing this stitch will create a line of interlocking threads on the edge of the fabric.

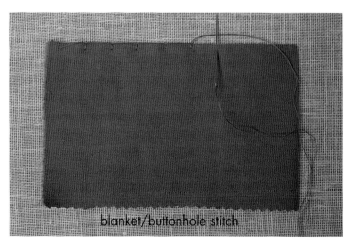

Gathering stitch

A long basting stitch usually sewn on a machine that is subsequently used to gather fabric. Two parallel rows of stitches will make the best, most even gathers. Gathering can also be done with a hand basting stitch.

To gather, place a pin at one end of the stitching. Take the long thread ends and weave a figure eight pattern around the pin to secure. (This keeps the thread from pulling out when you gather.) Move the fabric along the threads.

Staystitch

To stitch around the edge of the fabric to secure two or more layers together and/or to prohibit fabric from stretching and becoming misshapen.

Slipstitch or Hem Stitch

This stitch is for hemming or finishing any edge that requires an invisible, elegant resolve. This is a good stitch for hems and seam binding. Working from right to left, slide the needle into the folded edge of the fabric, picking up (at the same point) a single thread of the under fabric. Stitches should be 1/8" to 1/4" apart.

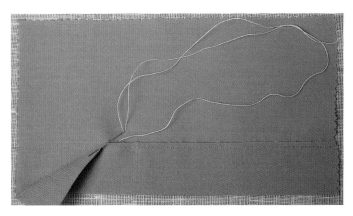

Stitch in the ditch

Using a completed seam as the stitch line, stitching along the seam from the right side to catch the layer underneath. Often used to finish bindings and casings.

Topstitch and Edgestitch

Stitching on the right side of the fabric that is meant to be seen. Topstitching can be functional or decorative. **Edgestitching** is a form of topstitching where the stitching is as close as possible to the edge.

Understitch

Creating an edge of fabric by enclosing a seam allowance in a fold, then understitching by machine or hand to prevent rolling.

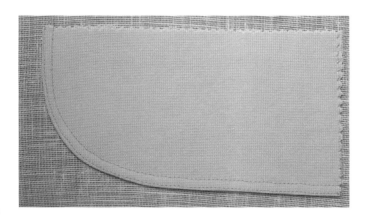

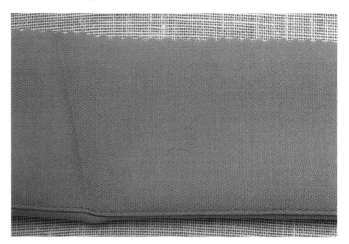

Beading

Single Beads

1. Thread your beading needle with a single strand of thread in a color that matches your fabric. Tie a knot at the end of the thread.
2. Come up through the right side of the fabric so that the knot is on the wrong side.
3. Put the bead on the needle and go back down through the fabric right by where you came up. Pull the thread tight.
4. Come back up through the fabric and go through the same bead again, repeating step 3.
5. Knot the thread on the wrong side, but don't cut it.
6. Move on to the next bead and repeat, knotting off after each bead until all single beads in an area are secure. ❏

Examples of beading single beads.

Beading Lines and Strands

Lines and strands are usually done with bugle beads. You can use lines of beads to make or accent a design or make short strands to use as fringe. Here's how to bead a line on fabric:

1. Thread the beading needle with a single strand of thread in a color that matches the fabric. Tie a knot at the end of the thread.
2. Starting on the wrong side of the fabric, come up through the fabric with the needle at the point where you want the line of beads to begin.
3. Pick up a bead on the needle and go back through the fabric where the bead ends. (The bead should now be lying flat on the fabric.)
4. Bring the needle up through the fabric at the first end of the bead and go through the bead again. Add the second bead on the needle without going through the fabric.
5. Go back down through the fabric at the other end of the second bead and come up through the fabric at the first end of the second bead.
6. Go through the second bead and add the third bead.
7. Continue in this manner until you have all of the beads in the desired line on the thread.
8. Knot the thread on the wrong side. **Do not** cut the thread.
9. Come back up through the fabric at the second end of the last bead. Go back through all the beads in the line again and knot off the thread. ❏

Examples of beading lines and strands.

Bias

About Bias

Cutting on the bias means to cut at a 45 degree angle to the grain line of a fabric. The bias is the diagonal (45 degree angle) between the straight grain and cross grain.

Finding the Bias

Follow these simple steps to locate true bias:

1. Pulling a thread on the cross grain.

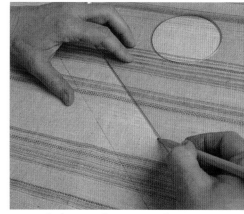

2. Mark the 45 degree angle.

1. Pull on the opposite diagonals to straighten the fabric. (Sometimes fabric is pulled "off grain" during processing.)
2. Pull a thread on the cross grain to find the true straight of grain line. [photo 1]
3. Fold the cross grain (usually 45") at one corner down the edge of the selvage. Use a straight edge and marking tool. I use a plastic right isosceles triangle to mark my 45 degree angle. [photo 2] *Option:* Position a gridded ruler along the cross grain and lengthwise grain (warp and weft) and draw a 2" square. Draw a line connecting the opposite corners and continue the line. This is true bias. [photo 3]

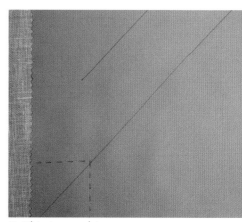

3. This is true bias.

Making Bias Binding

Bias binding is an easy, useful way to finish and accent at the same time. The advantage of cutting strips for binding on the bias is bias' inherent stretchability – bias binding will easily fit around curves without easing. In this book, bias strips are used frequently to make bindings for finishing the raw edges of projects and as trims.

Bias binding is made by cutting strips of fabric on the bias (45 degrees from the selvage edge) in straight lines. To determine how wide the bias strips need to be for the size binding you want, use this simple formula: Cut four times the finished width. For example, 1/2" visible finished binding is 2" cut width. (1/2" x 4 = 2)

It is easiest to cut one continuous strip of fabric the length that you require, but this is not always the most economical use of fabric. Piecing bias strips can make a little fabric go a long way. Piecing also can be a wonderful way to create a graphic-edged accent.

Continuous Bias

You can make a large amount of bias strips by piecing the fabric *before* cutting. Here's how:

1. Draw the diagonal lines at a 45 degree angle from the selvage.
2. Join the shorter ends of marked fabric, right sides together, with one strip width extending beyond the edge at each side. **Do not** align the corners. Instead, make sure one strip lines up with the next one over.
3. Stitch, using a 1/4" seam allowance. Press seams open.
4. Cut apart on the marked lines to make one long strip. [photo]

Bias Tape Makers

A bias tape maker is a metal device that folds bias strips to make bias binding. You feed a bias strip in one side, and press as it comes out folded on the other side. The resulting binding has two folded-in seam allowances and a fold to put over the edge, just like the bias binding you can buy at fabric stores. This is called double fold bias tape.

Binding with Double Fold Bias Tape

1. Unfold one edge of the bias tape and stitch to the edge of the project, stretching the binding slightly as you sew.
2. Fold binding back over the raw edge with the seam allowance enclosed. Stitch from the top side of the project on the edge or "in the ditch," making sure you catch the other side.

Bob's Bias Tape Maker

You can easily make your own bias tape maker. This super trick was passed on to us via Bob Trump, a tailor at The Rep Theatre of St. Louis. **Here's how:**

1. On a stable piece of fabric, draw two parallel lines the distance between which will be the width of the bias.
2. Then draw a set of three vertical lines to create two squares. The distance between these parallel lines is also the desired width of the bias.
3. Next, take a few hand stitches from point 1 to point 2, then a few more from point 3 to point 4, and next from point 5 to point 6. The stitches **must** be taken in this order – when you are finished you will have what looks like a Roman numeral XI.
4. To create the bias binding tape, feed bias strips of fabric through the "X" and the "I" (in that order), position the strips so that the fabric folds into bias tape. Press as you pull it along.

"French" Bias

A double-thickness bias strip works well for applications where you need wide bias binding, like blanket binding or bias facing. You need six times the desired finished width for this. Start with a long strip of bias.

Continued on next page

Continuous Bias

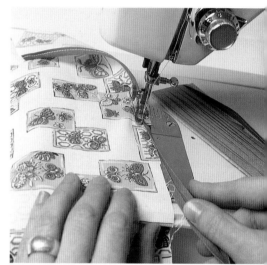

Applying double fold bias binding to an edge.

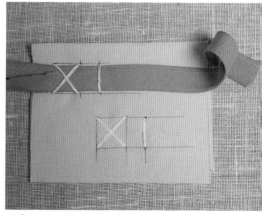

Bob's Bias Tape Maker

Continued from page 121

1. Fold a short end back about 1/2" to create a clean edge. Fold the strip in half lengthwise.
2. With wrong sides together, press.
3. Baste the raw edges together.
4. Place the raw edge of the bias strip along the raw edge of the project, with right sides together.
5. Stitch through all layers, using a seam allowance the same width you want the binding to be.
6. Fold the bias strip over to the wrong side of the fabric. Press. Hand stitch the back side.

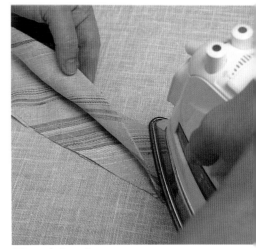
"French Bias"

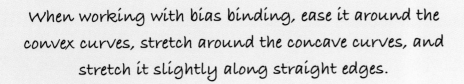
When working with bias binding, ease it around the convex curves, stretch around the concave curves, and stretch it slightly along straight edges.

Making Bias Piping and Bias-Covered Cord

Bias piping can be inserted in any seam for a decorative effect. It's a favorite for pillows, slipcovers, and upholstery. You can buy readymade piping in fabric stores, but it's easy to make your own – simply cover cord with bias strips. (Piping made this way is called cording.) The cord is available in a variety of diameters and is sold by the yard.

1. Cut bias strips of fabric, seaming as needed to achieve the length you need.
2. Place cord inside the fabric and wrap the cord, aligning the edges of the bias strip, wrong sides together.
3. Stitch along the cord as closely as possible, using the zipper foot of your machine.

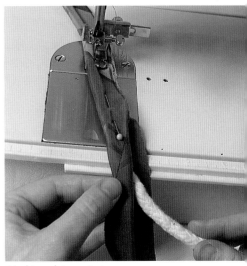
Making bias piping

Bias-covered cord is used for straps, belts, curtain tie-backs, and trim. To make your own, use the same type of round cord used to make piping and cut and seam enough bias strips to cover the amount of cord you need.

1. Seam and turn a tube from the bias strips whose circumference will accommodate the circumference of the cord.
2. Attach a bodkin (a tool you can buy at fabric stores) to one end of the cord and pull it through the tube.

Optional handsewing method:

1. Cut a bias strip the width of the tube you wish to make plus 1/2".
2. Press each long edge under 1/4".
3. Wrap bias strip around cord and stitch by hand with matching thread.

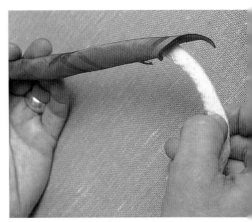
Bias-covered cord

French Seam

This seam is finished on both sides and hides the raw edge. It is especially suited for fabrics you can see through or delicate fabrics that ravel easily. I prefer it on lingerie and fine clothing.

Making a French Seam

1. Stitch fabric with wrong sides together with a 3/8" seam allowance.
2. Press seam flat and trim to 1/8".
3. With right sides together, stitch again using another 3/8" seam allowance, enclosing the previously made seam inside.
4. Press the seam allowance to one side.

Mitered Corners

Simple Mitered Corner

If you choose to miter a corner on an applied pocket or any other detail, this is a simple method.

1. At the corner of the turned back seam allowance, make a diagonal fold. Press with your iron.
2. Open the fold and stitch along the crease line.
3. Trim the seam closely and press open.
4. Turn the hem under and stitch by hand or machine.

A simple mitered corner, before turning.

To apply a continuous strip of fabric or ribbon around corners you can miter it before it is attached or miter it as you sew it on.

continued from page 123

Mitered Trim BEFORE YOU APPLY

1. Press all the seam allowances on the band to the inside.
2. Lay the trim band on the project and mark the corner. [**photo 1**]
3. Fold the trim band back at a 45 degree angle. Press. [**photo 2**]
4. Unfold and stitch along the creased line. [**photo 3**]
5. Trim closely along the stitching line and press open. You can now attach the trim to the project with perfect mitered corners! ❏

1. Marking the corner.

2. The trim band, folded back and pressed.

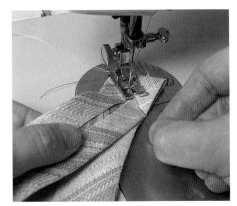

3. Stitching the corner along the creased line.

Mitered Trim AS YOU SEW

This works best when the trim has a finished edge, e.g., a ribbon or purchased bias tape.

1. Pin the trim into place. Edgestitch along the inner edge.
2. Fold the trim back and crease, then fold again at a 45 degree angle and press.
3. Unfold trim and stitch along through the pressed crease, stitching through the trim and the underlayer at once. [**photo 1**]
4. Trim close to the seam and press open. Continue stitching around project. Edgestitch around the outside of the trim to finish. [**photo 2**]

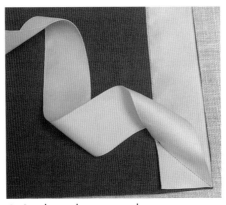

1. Stitching the trim to the corner.

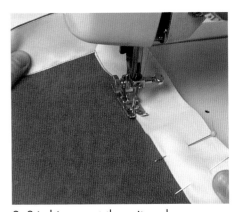

2. Stitching past the mitered corner.

Mitered Double Hem

This is a good way to hem a napkin, a placemat, or a tablecloth.

1. On all four sides, fold down a 1/2" hem of fabric to the wrong side. Press.
2. Fold under 1/2" again, and press.
3. Unfold the fabric. Trim across each corner to make a nice miter. [**photo 1**]
4. Fold the first 1/2" down again to the wrong side.

5. At the corners, place right sides of the hem together and stitch across the corners at a 45 degree angle to the edge of the fabric. [**photo 2**] Trim off the extra fabric at the corner triangles and press the seams open.
6. Turn the second hem under 1/2" on the wrong side of the fabric, and press.
7. Edgestitch the hem. [**photo 3**]

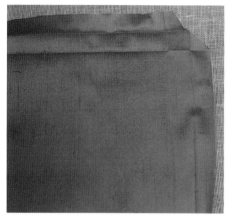

1. The pressed double hem, unfolded and trimmed.

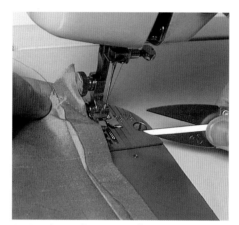

2. Stitching the mitered corner.

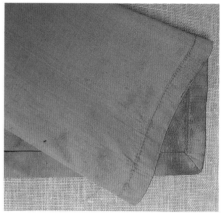

3. A finished corner.

Quilting

Stitching through multiple layers of fabric to create a design or a motif. For the best effect, add a layer of light batting between the layers. Mark the desired quilting pattern with a straight edge or ruler so that the stitching increments will be precise.

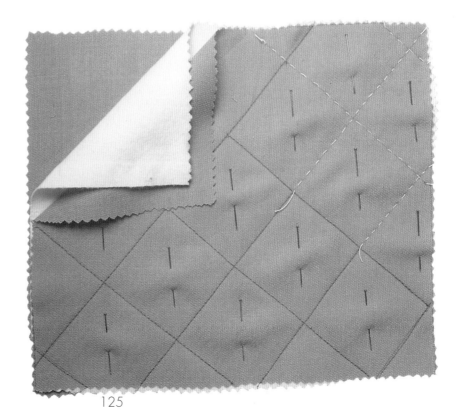

Metric Conversion Chart

Inches	MM	CM
1/8	3	.3
1/4	6	.6
3/8	10	1.0
1/2	13	1.3
5/8	16	1.6
3/4	19	1.9
7/8	22	2.2
1	25	2.5
1-1/4	32	3.2
1-1/2	38	3.8
1-3/4	44	4.4
2	51	5.1
3	76	7.6
4	102	10.2
5	127	12.7
6	152	15.2
7	178	17.8
8	203	20.3
9	229	22.9
10	254	25.4
11	279	27.9
12	305	30.5

YARDS TO METERS

Yards	Meters
1/8	.11
1/4	.23
3/8	.34
1/2	.46
5/8	.57
3/4	.69
7/8	.80
1	.91
2	1.83
3	2.74
4	3.66
5	4.57
6	5.49
7	6.40
8	7.32
9	8.23
10	9.14

Index

Index